San Diego Visions

San Diego Visions

Written & Illustrated
by
Bro Halff

Simpler Gifts Press, LLC
San Diego

Published in 2021 by Simpler Gifts Press, LLC
and Bro Halff Gallery Hawaii, LLC

For information, address the publishers:

Simpler Gifts Press, LLC
1050 Rosecrans Street, Suite D
San Diego, California 92106

Bro Halff Gallery Hawaii, LLC
1706 Keoniloa Place
Koloa, Hawaii 96756

Library of Congress Card Catalog Number
ISBN 978-1-885238-17-7

This book is dedicated to Dave and Ryan,
who have given me my fondest memories of San Diego.

San Diego has always welcomed the practical and the visionary. Perhaps because of its relative isolation from the rest of the country, the city has nurtured individuals and endeavors that have made the city as interesting as it is beautiful. This book, along with its companion volume, *San Diego Days*, is my effort to capture both the beauty and the sometimes-elusive spirit of San Diego and its environs.

I had the pleasure of living in San Diego for two decades, from 1986 until 2006. My art gallery is still there. Most visitors to San Diego, and many residents, may have little idea of the intricate interaction of idealism and pragmatism that from its earliest days has distinguished this city. Even in the year 1769, when Gaspar de Portolá built the San Diego Presidio, or garrison, Franciscan Fathers Junipero Serra, Juan Vizcaíno, and Fernando Parrón established the first of California's twenty-one missions, San Diego de Alcalá, just a few miles from the Presidio. The mission was designed to convert and serve the Kumeyaay indigenous people, who did not always welcome the ministerial regimen of the Franciscan fathers, against whom they rebelled in 1775. Despite the sometimes-flawed ministry of the Franciscans, their spiritual dedication was genuine. The friars believed that they were leading unenlightened native peoples to a European system of faith in God, hard work, and organized communal existence.

This contrast between the spiritual and the practical concerns of humankind has been writ large in the history of San Diego. For example, Point Loma was once the home of one of the country's most fascinating and disciplined spiritual communes. Katherine Tingley, a social worker and prominent member of the semi-religious Theosophical Society, founded Lomaland, on Point Loma, in 1900, when she moved one branch of the Theosophical Society's headquarters from New York City to Point Loma. The schools and university that she established, on this windswept peninsula overlooking the Pacific Ocean, taught young children, as well as adult theosophists, in a system of spiritual and physical discipline that was both rigorous and mystical. The spartan lifestyle and intellectual intensity that the society demanded of its followers generated some unintended consequences. Many of the youngsters who attended the Theosophical Society's school for young children went on to become the leading entrepreneurs and civic leaders of San Diego, in the early to mid-twentieth century. These pillars of society recalled in later years that the ardor and rigor of their early education gave them the discipline and zeal that enabled them to promote and build San Diego's economy into one of national caliber.

This tradition of vision and enterprise has been upheld numerous times in the history of San Diego. T. Claude Ryan was a forestry patrol pilot who dreamt of building an airline and an airplane manufacturing company. He founded Ryan Airlines in 1925, with service between San Diego and Los Angeles. He eventually sold Ryan Airlines, to finance his Ryan Aeronautical Corporation, which built the *Spirit of Saint Louis*, Charles Lindbergh's single-engine plane, flown on the first solo transatlantic flight. Ryan's subsequent companies went on to build a number of aircraft, especially trainers, until he sold his last enterprise to Teledyne in 1969. His designs influenced many other commercial and military aircraft manufacturers, and also contributed significantly to the evolution of pilotless drones.

Over the years, as I came to know more and more of San Diego's hidden treasures, I sought to portray, in poetry and watercolors, their sometimes-elusive charms. I never ceased to be amazed by the quiet gardens and inviting cottages that graced many of the city's older neighborhoods, from Point Loma to Ocean Beach, Pacific Beach, and La Jolla, and from Coronado to Little Italy, Bankers Hill, Hillcrest, Mission Hills, North Park, Claremont, and Golden Hills. Large suburbs flank San Diego to the north, south, and east, but they are communities that generally have burgeoned more recently than did the core of San Diego. While these newer neighborhoods have their own charms and histories, my attention has always been focused on the parts of San Diego that grew up primarily between 1900 and 1970. Their diversity is a testament to San Diego's tradition of welcoming both dreamers and doers. Both types of human endeavor frequently have been manifested in individuals who came to be seen as visionaries, when they converted their dreams into startling new realities.

San Diego also has been the home of superb artists, especially some members of the Early California Art school of art. These artists settled in San Diego in the early years of the twentieth century. They produced artworks of dramatic beauty, capturing what was still largely a land of unspoiled landscapes and intimate cityscapes. Alfred Mitchell, Maurice Braun, Charles Fries, and Charles Reiffel, among others, all brought to life the San Diego "back country" and coastline. Shortly after I moved to San Diego, I came to know their work, through my friendship with an authority on Early California Art, Merika Gopaul. These painters inspired me to seek out unexplored, as well as familiar, scenes that were to become my haunts, for over twenty years.

These precious sites, sometimes far from modern urban life, along with the lives of many people whom I met and observed in San Diego, inspired me to paint and write the work that you find in this book. For me, San Diego will always remain a generous refuge, where insight and observation of life blossom, even in the middle of a bustling American city. I hope that you will enjoy my visions of this unique corner of the United States, a place where personal dreams and grand enterprises both have found fertile soil in which to flourish.

At Ease

A quiet day
beside the harbor
rests
in subdued sunlight,
while ships
come and go,
and a fleet of clouds
find a calm harbor,
in which
they raise their sails
to run
before the wind,

while in the distance
mountains
hoist
their purple
sentinel flags,
waving
to a horizon
where islands
nap
in armchairs
fashioned of waves.

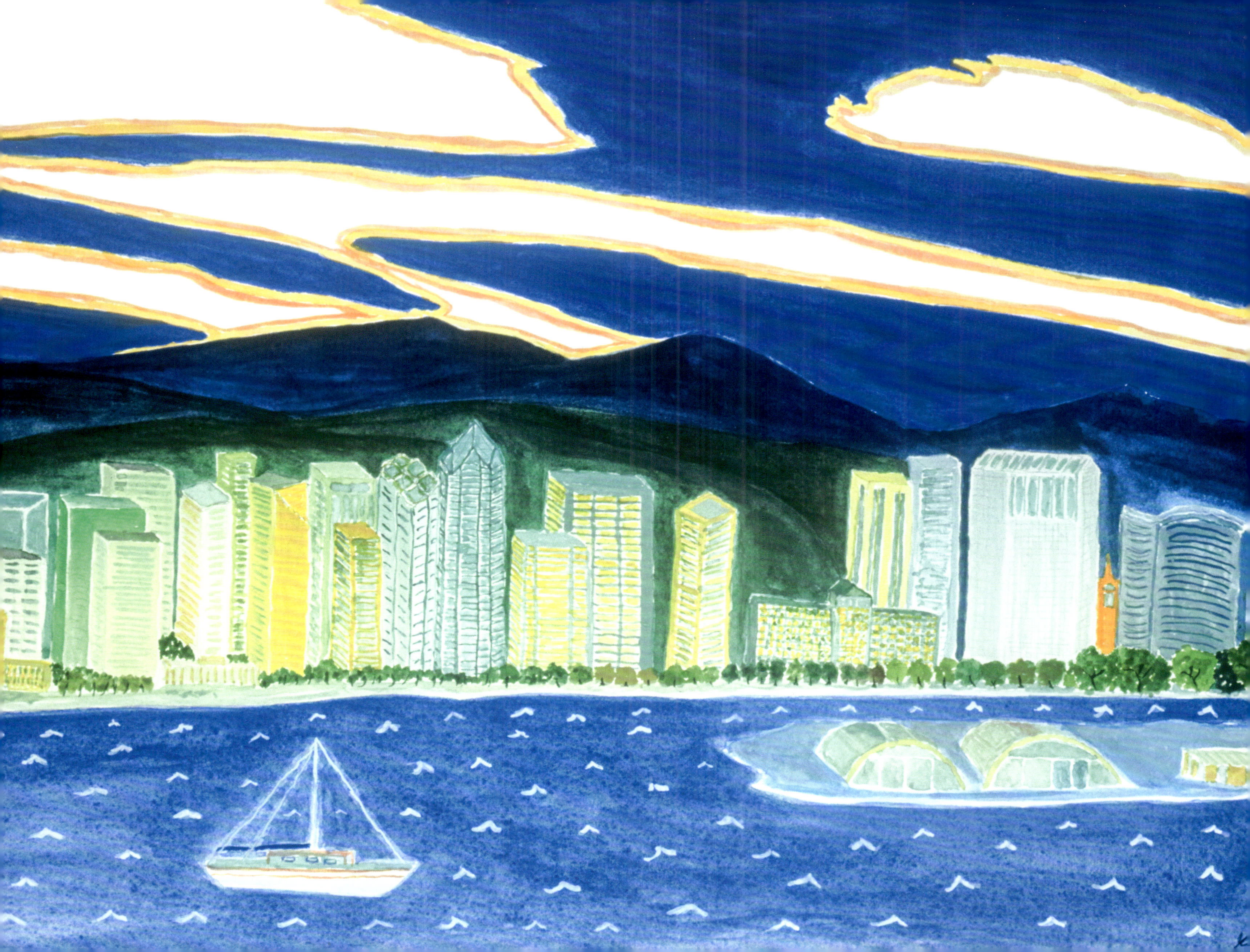

Partners

Listening to the waves
dance all night
with the shore,
you dream
of a cloud
that crosses
the horizon,
discovering
an island
that has settled down
with an ocean
that is light
on its feet.

Grace in Motion

A limping woman
trudges
against the wind
toward a glassy-eyed
all-night restaurant –
pressing her way
across the parking lot,
with her lumpy body
bundled
in a brown gabardine coat,
she outstretches
her firm hand
to a mirror-bright door
that, ignoring all others,
has asked her
for this dance.

Sky High

Three trees
in spring,
festooning a hillside,
raise their green
lanterns,
lit by morning light,
which climbs the slope
to overlook
a far canyon,
above which the sky
hangs up its linens,
to wave
at young hands,
shaking
pompoms
that whisper
of runaway
victories.

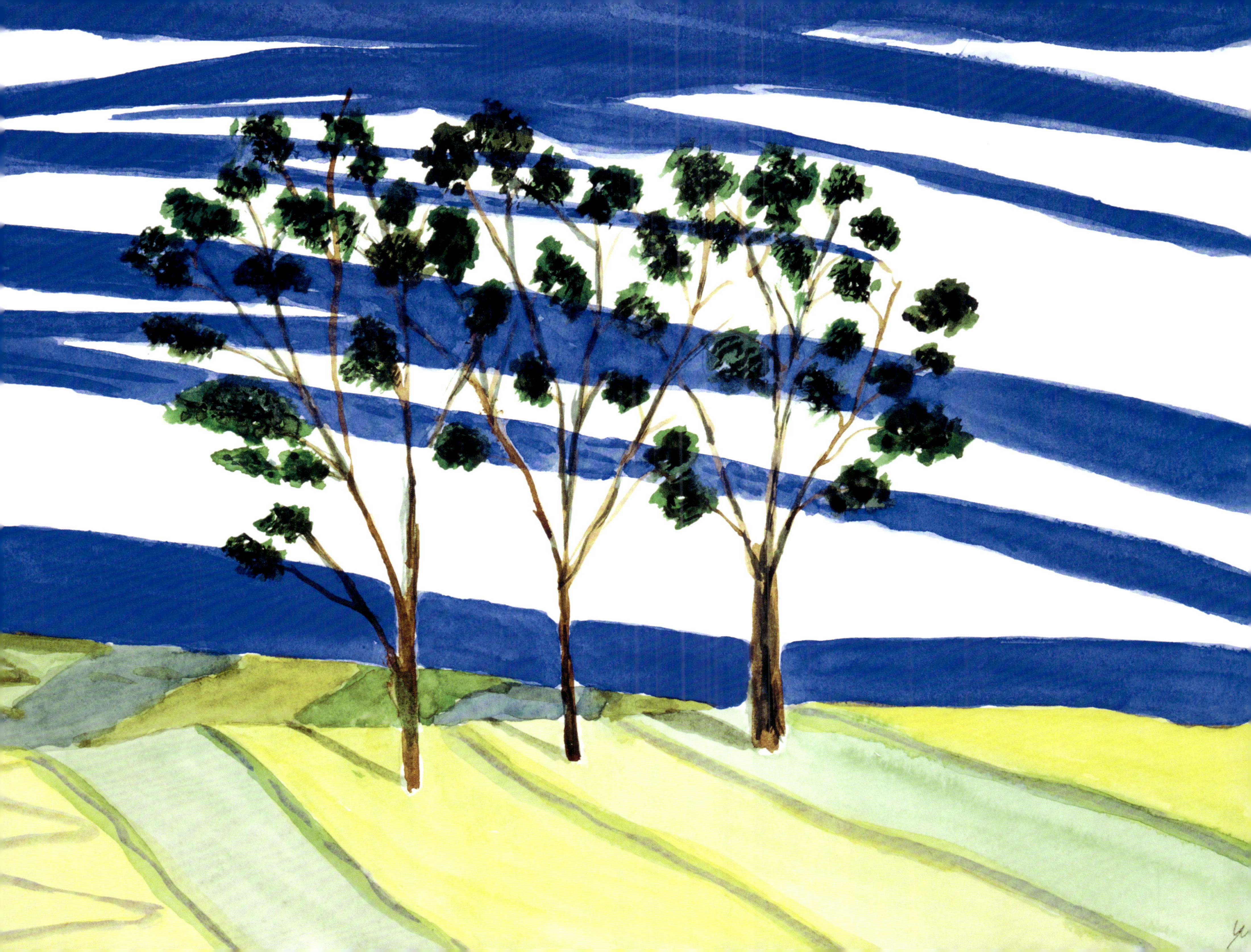

Free to Laugh

The reflection
of an American flag
ripples
in a bright-eyed
window,
saluting
an open-armed sky,
and an ocean
whose waves
kick up
their heels.

Fiery Wrinkles

An old man
with a cane
and a wispy gray beard
swaggers
through a crowd,
undaunted
by strangers –
making his way
down the sidewalk,
he taps
on the cement,
awakening the earth
beneath its gray skin,
warning the pavement
that one day
its cracks
will sprout
grass-green
whiskers.

Catching Fire

Light
at the end
of the world
signals
the ocean,
the bay,
the soft hills
that encircle
the waves –
together they hold
their silent
vigil,
their wait
for westering
sunlight
that pours out a pool,
where pelicans
search
for sleek swimmers.

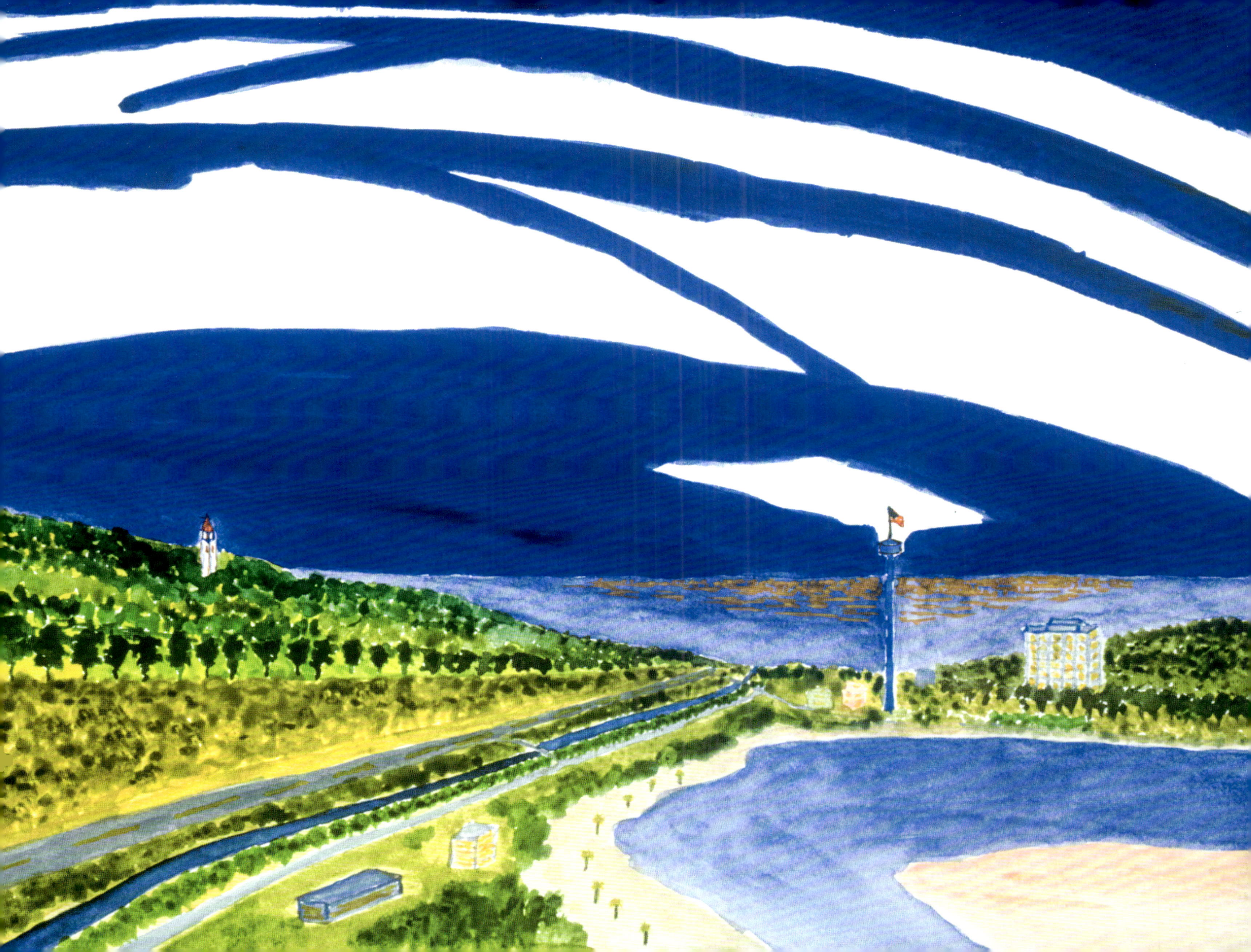

Sharing a Snooze

Soft hills
stretch out
at dusk –
in the fading
light,
they doze
beside one another,
peaceful bedfellows
who snuggle
with their shadows.

Measuring the Middle

An old man,
laughing
as he stares
out the window,
stands up
to watch
a cardinal
take flight,
then opens
his door
and gazes
at a tall pine,
no more
than a perch
for a bird
with an eye
on a worm
and a cat.

An Autumn Salute

A solitary
pine tree,
nestled
among the rocks,
raises
its boughs
to a canopy
of sunlight,
while behind it
a host
of green and yellow leaves
lose sight
of everything,
except the blue and white
flag
of the sky.

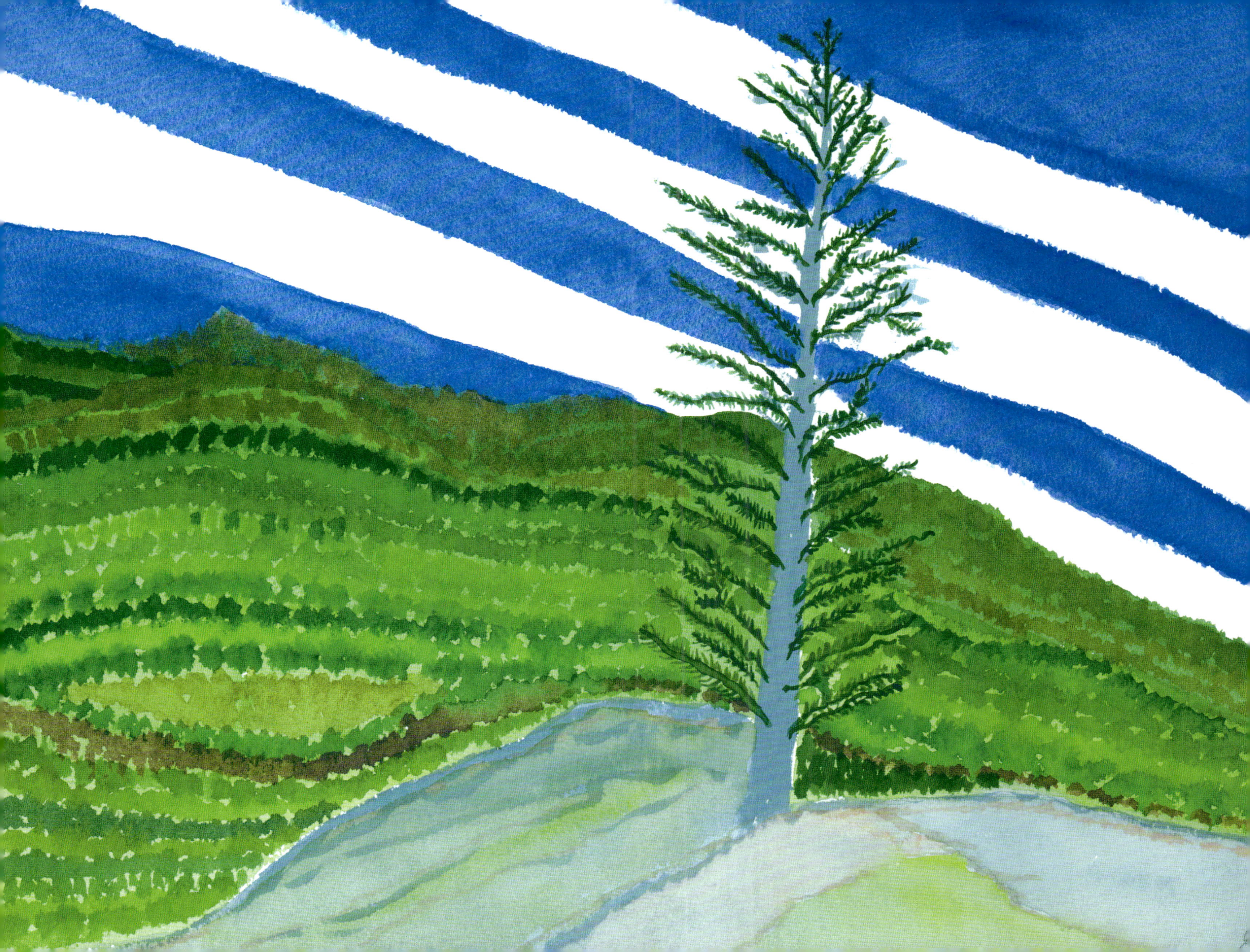

Making Change

Sunlight
on the ocean,
a golden path
with no fixed
destination,
crosses
the horizon
and continues
its journey,
meandering
away
from a green,
corduroy-coated
coast,
which has settled
down
to go dancing
under a dime
of a moon.

Greeting the Light

Late light
waits
at the end of the street –
you point it out
to your father,
just as he leaves
your house –
"Look at the sunlight, Dad,
even at this hour,"
you tell him,
and he sits
on your front porch bench
and looks;
but he already has seen it,
and it is you
who must recognize
fire
just beyond
the horizon.

Reunions

The space
where sky
meets sea
is sacred,
by timeless decree –
two infinite
spirits,
a single
story –
the light
comes calling
to reveal
their glory.

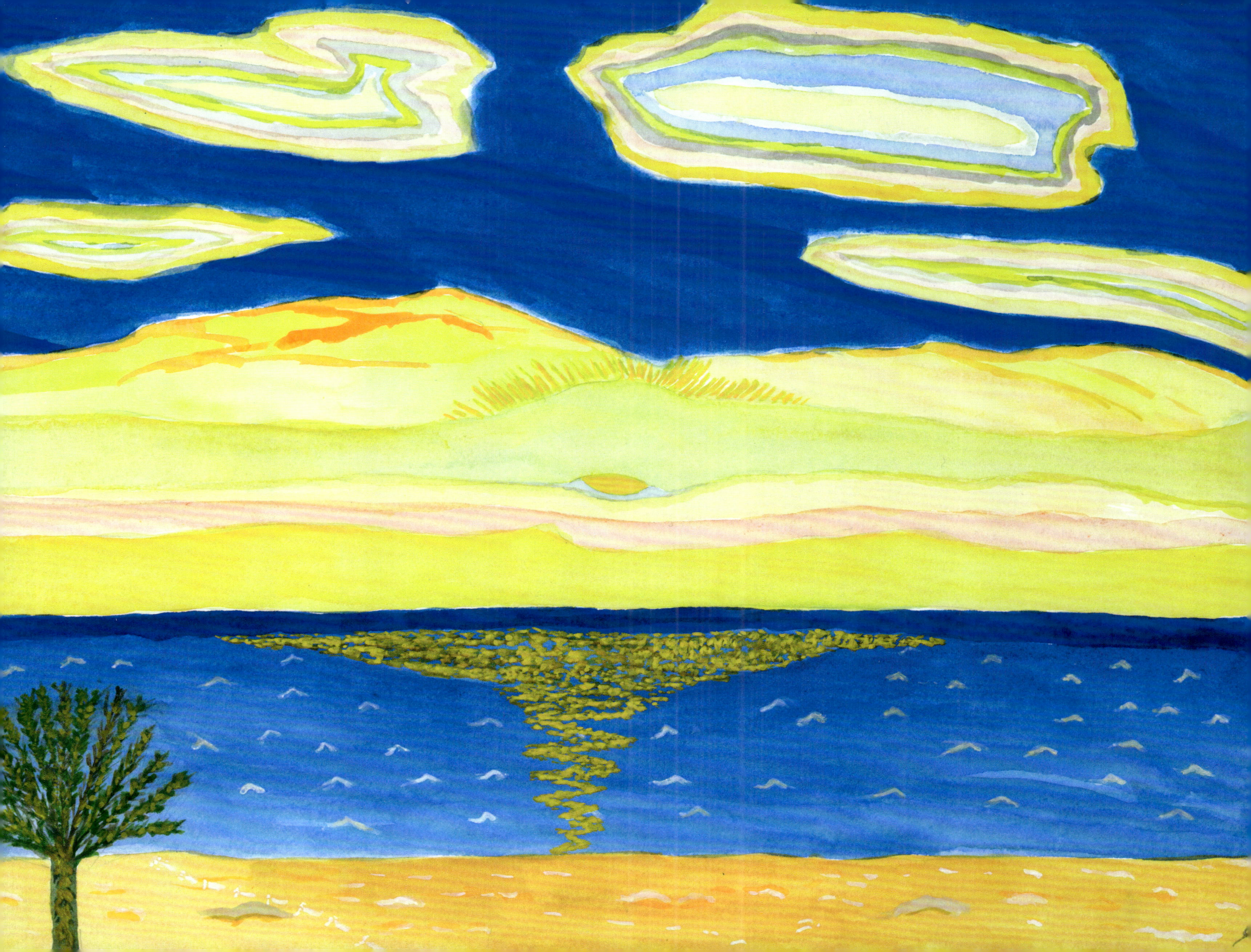

Mending the Afternoon

The bright coastline
in sunlight
rests
on a brilliant day,
while the hills
tumble down
to the ocean,
and the clouds
ring out their shadows,
as they move
from the sea
to the land,
scaling
nearby mountains,
which they cover
with purple
patches.

Counting on Surprises

A rugged man
walks northward
along the beach,
taking in
the ocean,
the cliffs,
the breakers,
as they somersault,
all in perfect order,
all in his past –
before him the road
waits
to astound him.

Lo and Behold

A road
snakes its way
around a green
hillside,
beneath which the rainbow cliffs
and the surf-necklaced ocean
bed down,
while at the horizon
two islands
wade
in a pool
of golden light,
squandered
in winter
to set
the sky
on its ear.

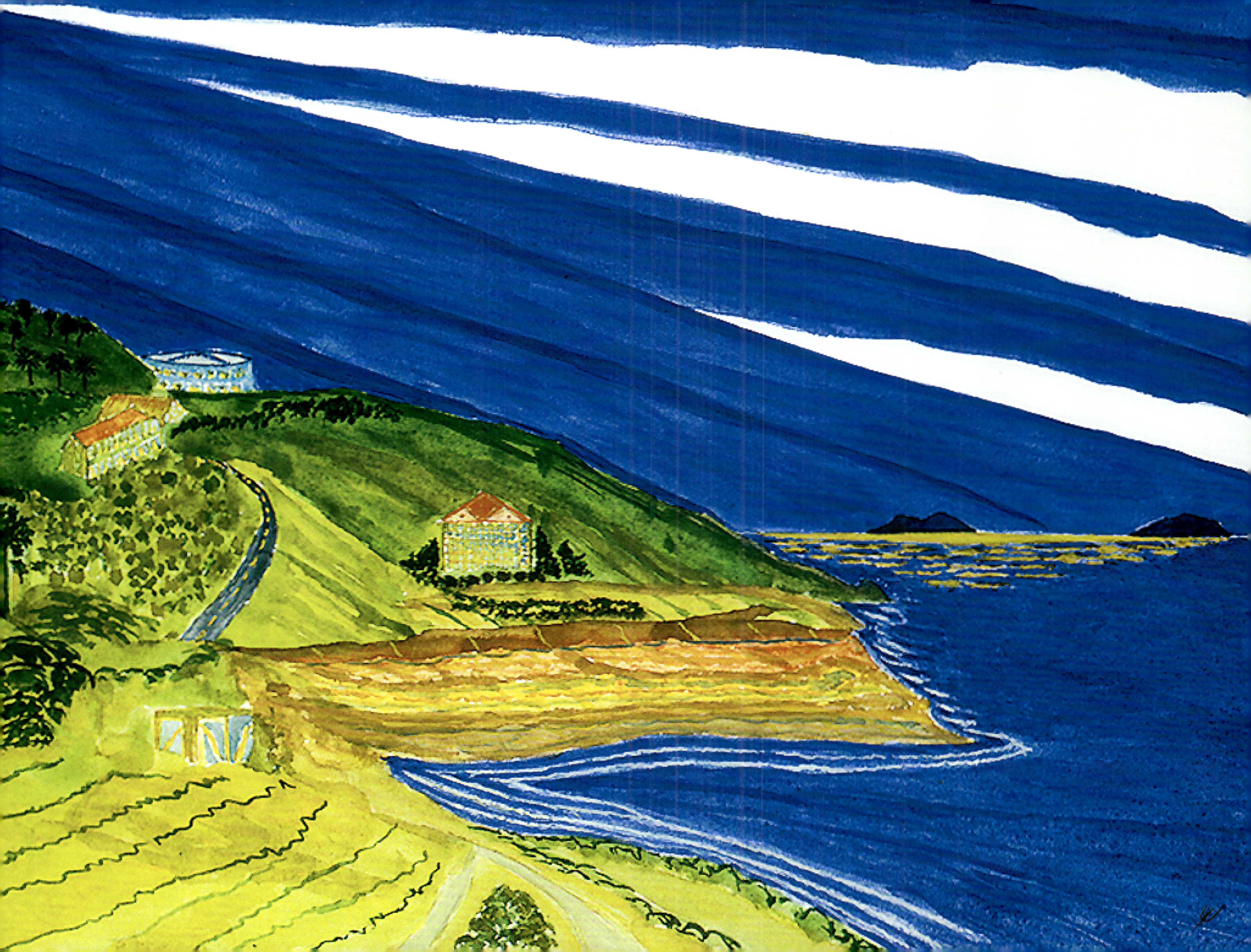

Conversations

The mountains and ocean
confer
together,
meeting
on sandy shores;
chatting,
they ignore
the overarching sky,
which whispers
to its clouds
of islands
that know
how to keep
a secret.

Better Late Than Never

At last
the old lady
coughs up
her secret –
behave yourself,
but have some fun,
before it's too late!

After all these years,
she spills
the beans –
who would imagine
that decades
of self-discipline
would lead her
to throw caution
to the wind?

She slumps back
in her chair
and rests,
closing
her eyes,
while you,
standing
dumbstruck,
pray that your vitamins
will work
miracles
today.

On the Rim

A small park
at the hem
of the ocean
embroiders
the shore
with the beads
and buttons
and porcelain
and fans
and shells
of its Pacific
past –

dragons
writhe,
while dolphins
leap
over rainbows,
and tigers
on teacups
stalk
jade-green mountains,
in a temple of trees
that wave
to a breeze
from the Orient.

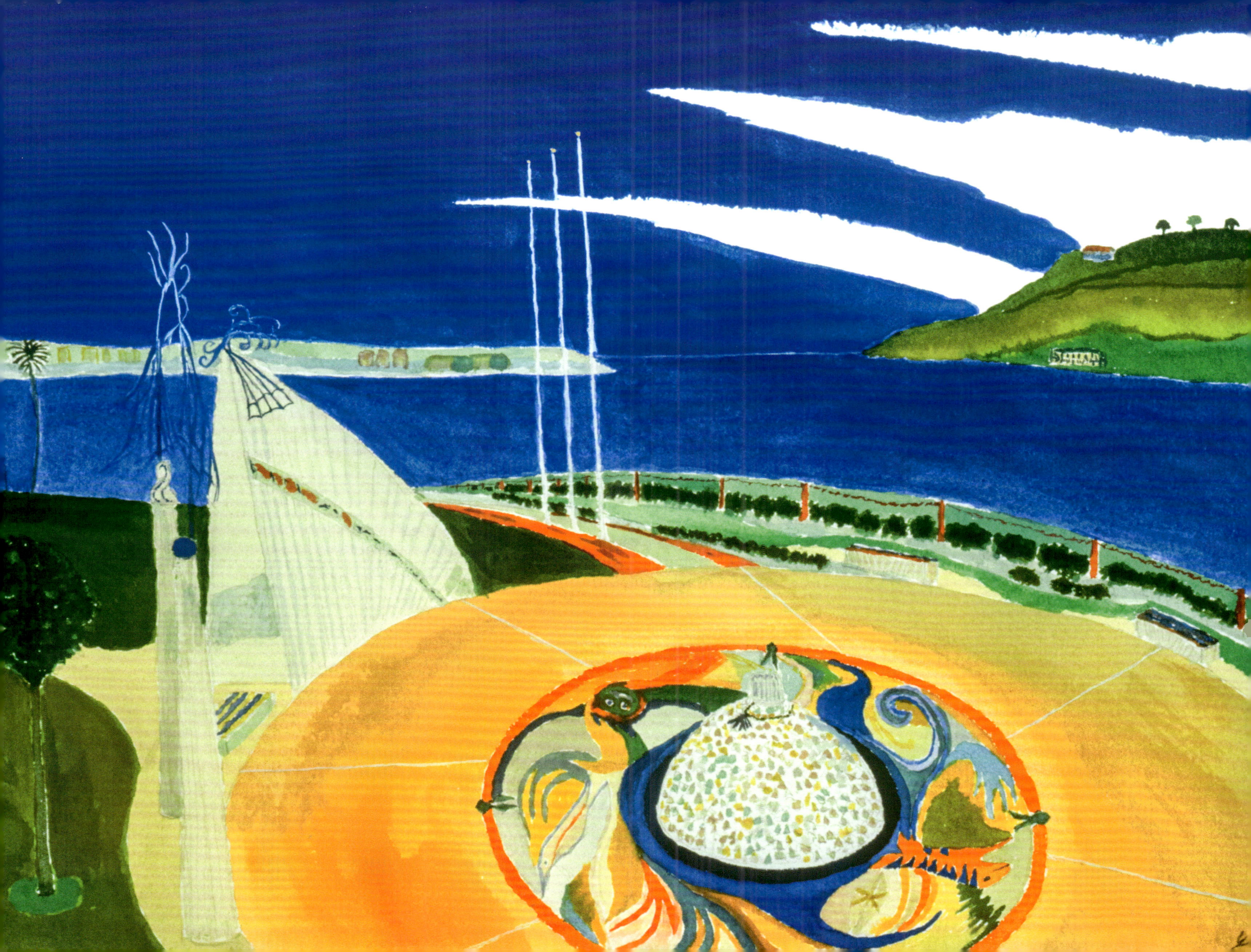

Calm Westerlies

At last
the sky clears,
and the coast
comes into view,
as the scars
of winter
heal up –
a thin woman
laughs
her womp-womp
laugh,
and the last
of the storm clouds
go on sale
as cotton candy.

Partners

Clouds
above the ocean
plant
their shadow islands,
then drift away
on a sunny day,
bearing with them
their cauliflower
gardens.

Gliding Away

Beyond the stern coast,
beyond the green
headlands,
the ocean
takes flight,
with purple
feathers
lifting
its lighthearted
wings.

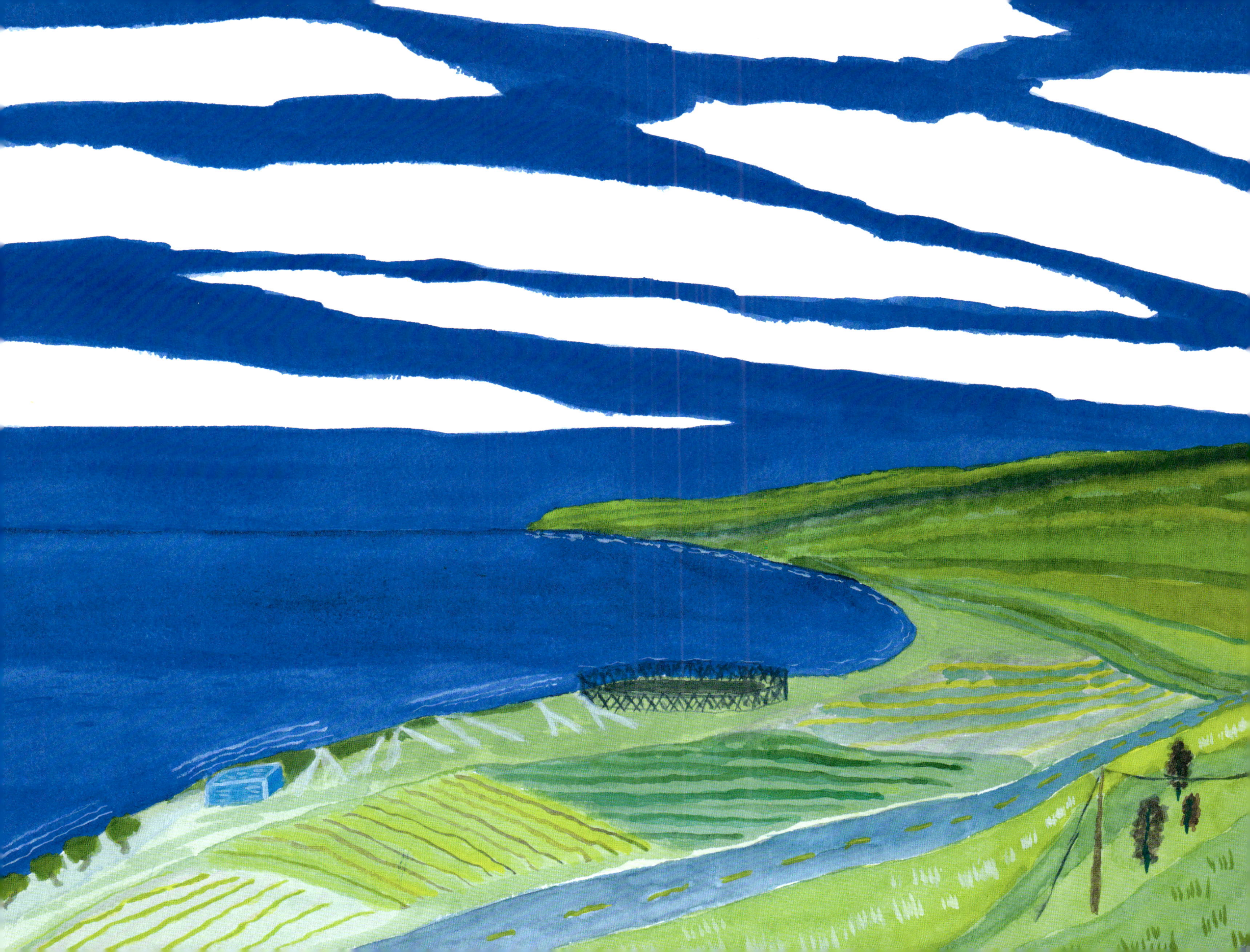

Nowhere to Hide

The woman
gathers
wild lilies
on a windy day,
in memory
of her sister –
how they dance
in her hands,
before
pretending
to sit primly
in a crystal-clear
vase.

Rebirth

A simpler day,
remembered,
slips
into silence,
and then,
awakening
to the laughter
of today,
dances
in the memory
and calls out
to a friend,
who recalls
your crooked smile,
and the calendar
that you looked for
in the clothes dryer.

Luckily,
it was not
tumbling there.

Polite Conversation

An elderly
Japanese man,
sitting
at an outdoor
table,
smiles
at his nervous-faced
daughter,
then pats
her hand,
as he waits
for a cloud's shadow
to swim
across a long pool,
leaving behind
a water lily's
unfurled
green doily.

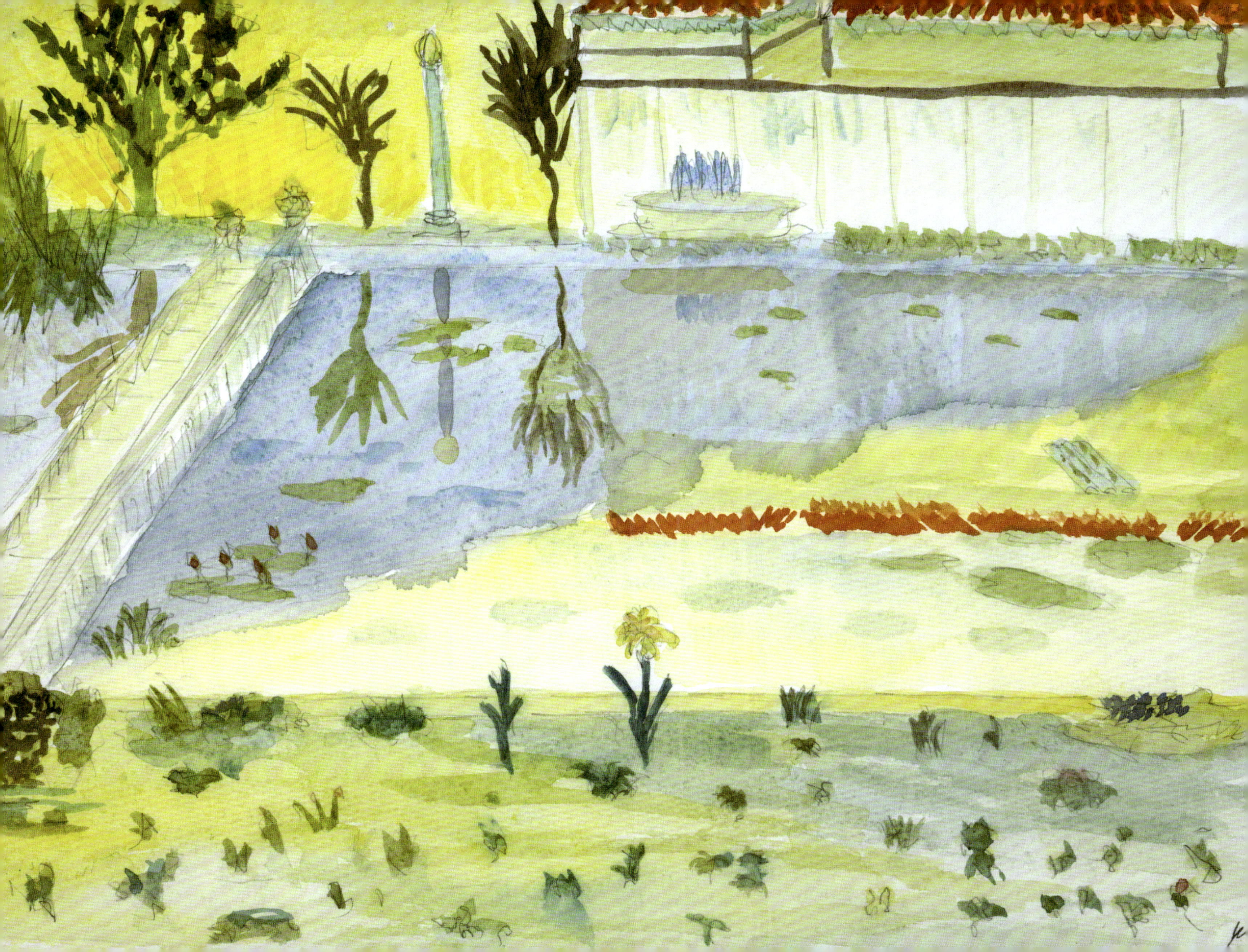

Bridesmaids

Fruit trees
in bloom
in January,
early believers
in lavender paradise,
give you hope
for a ramshackle
year,
when words
are your only
neighbors,
and the sky
is a skeptical
gray –
in early light,
the blossoms soften
a steel canopy,
until it glimmers
with blue patches,
above a premature
wedding bouquet
tossed
to the wind.

Coming to Terms

A quiet valley
beneath the mountains
settles in
for a day of rest,
while the peaks,
under clouds,
soften their hearts
to spring
rain.

Looking Up

Late light
on the mountains
etches them
into purple profiles,
busts
of ancient
emperors –
or are they
dusty-browed
philosophers,
who have fallen
asleep
at dusk,
and will awaken
at dawn,
with new smiles
on their kindly-carved
faces?

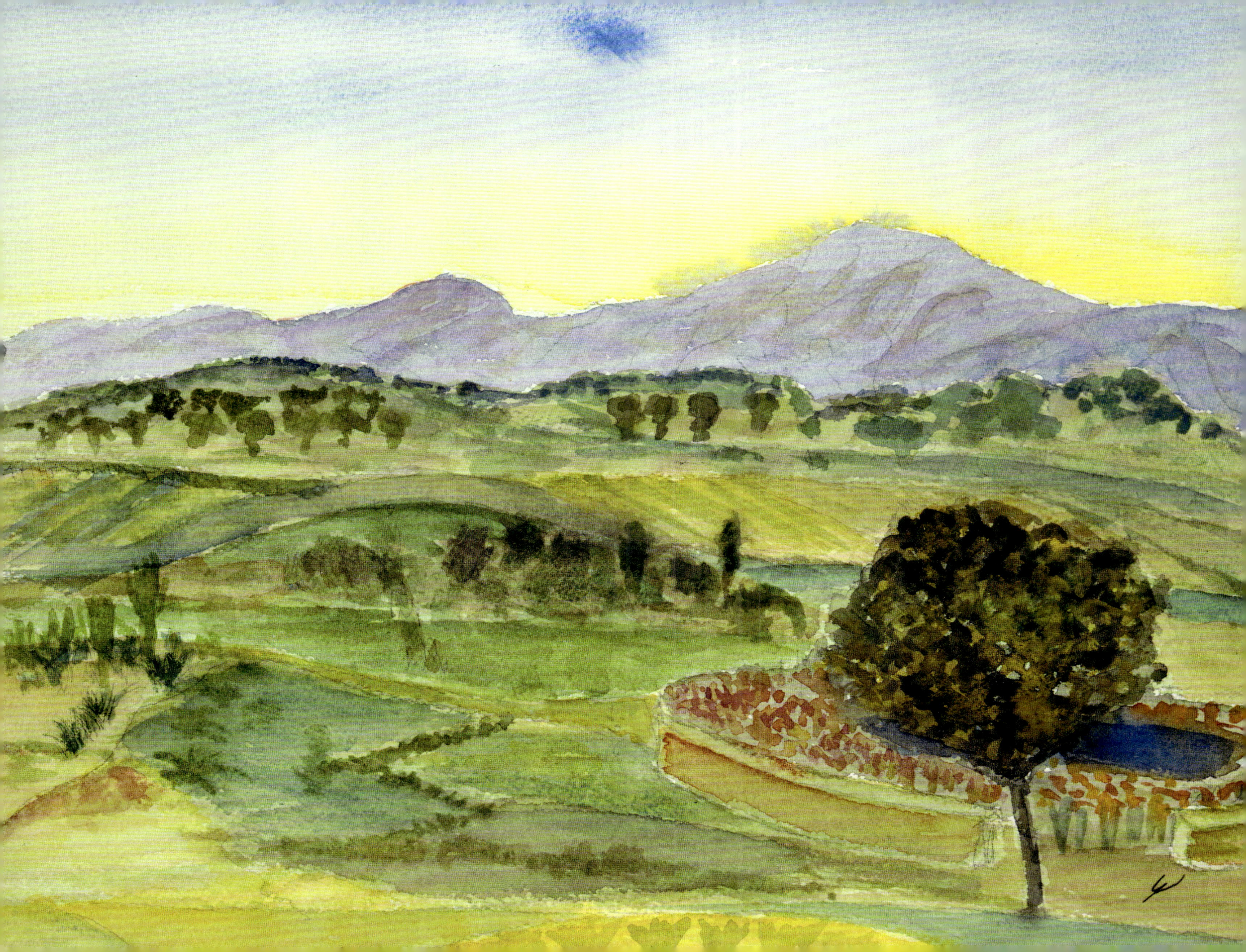

Ground Swell

The sailboat
under a perfect
cerulean blue sky
rides
the swell
and lets it
pass by,
then hoists high
its sail
and sets out
for a calm
harbor.

A Deep Laugh

A submarine
plies its way
across the ocean,
bracing the waves
and the bouncing
shafts of sunlight –
leaving its wake
to follow
its path,
it longs
to dive
and shake hands
with fishes.

Holding Its Breath

A sub base
rests
beneath the last
promontory,
pointing out
toward an ocean
that sleeps
soundly,
with air bubbles
tickling
its belly.

Sub Base, Point Loma

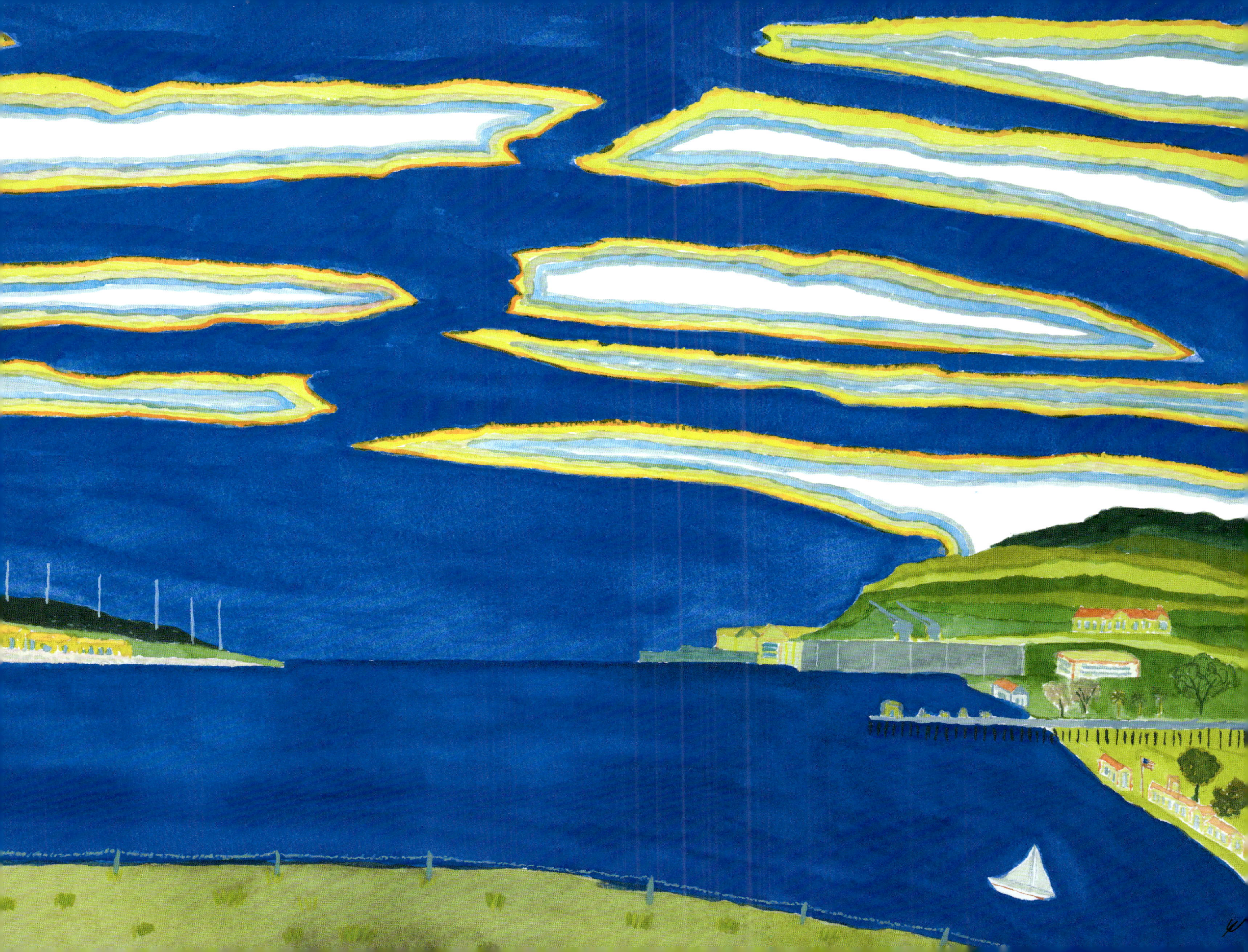

Hide and Seek

Fog,
playing
tag
with the coast,
blindfolds it
with the softest
of gauzes,
then pulls aside
the bandage,
leaving the land
clear-sighted,
gazing
at the bluest
of skies,
with no wool
pulled
over its eyes,
and the memory
of a trickster's
soft touch.

After the Party

A pasty-faced sky
passes out
on a gray afternoon –
after a night
of high-flying fireworks,
the fog
scrubs clean
the hillsides,
while the ocean
nibbles
on beaches –
all that remains
of the bright-eyed
dawn
is an island
of blue sky
that dances
at dusk
with wallflower
stars.

Spring Romances

Soft clouds
above the ocean
redden
and turn gold
at dusk,
then bed down
above the aquamarine
waves,
which doze
with their shadows,
as the sun
slips away,
leaving behind
sails
that answer
the whispers
of breezes.

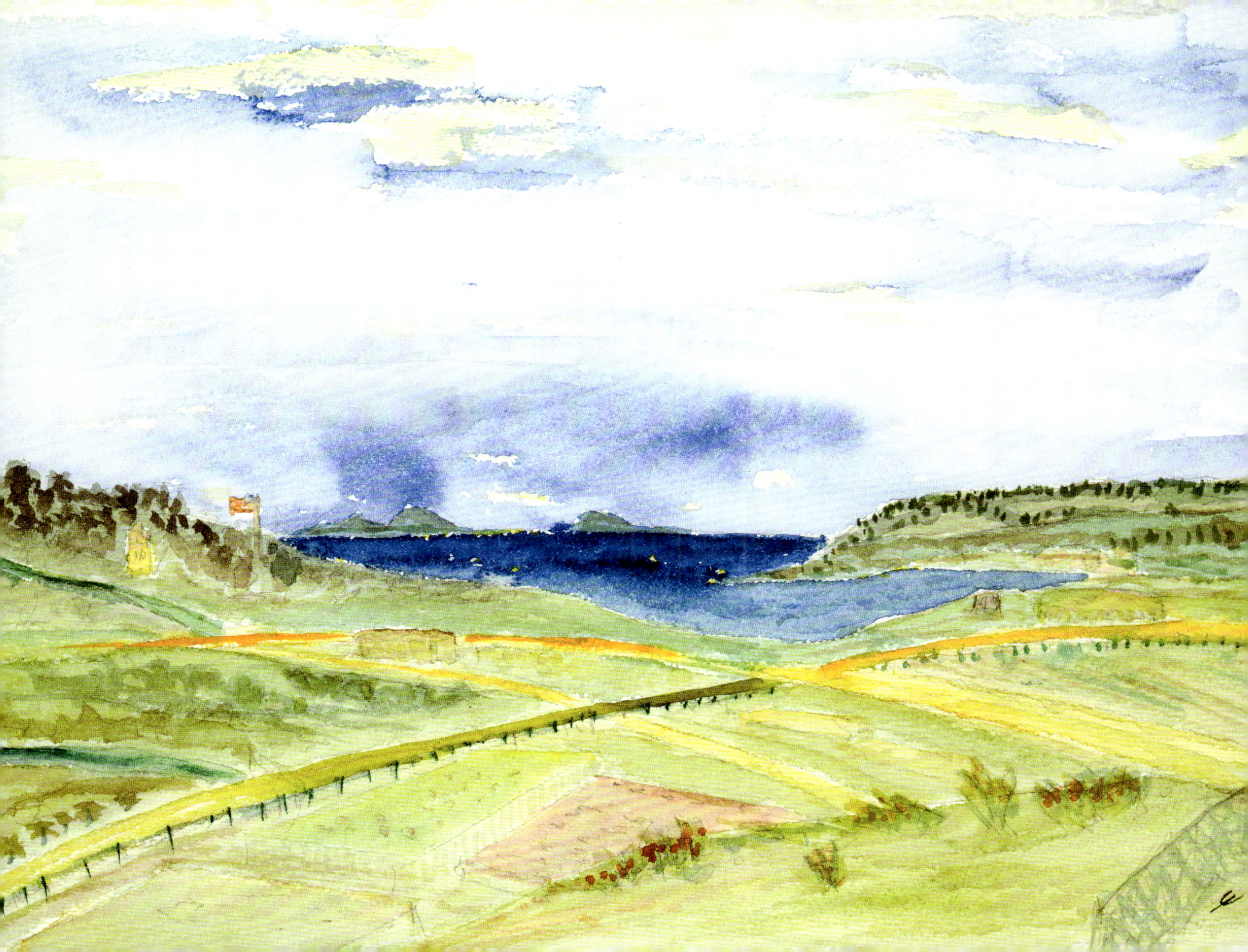

Chance Encounters

Waves
in the ocean,
plying their way
home,
cross the horizon
and discover
a new shore,
a stranger
whom they will meet
and welcome,
not seeking others
in the calm afternoon,
as the waves
make their way
across the ocean,
content
to meet islands
that insist
that they remember
how to swim.

A Summer Romance

The quiet ocean,
outstretching
its arms,
inspires the horizon
to embrace
an island
of fog.

Escape Artists

Islands at dusk,
lingering
beyond the reach
of the land
and the sky,
set out
for sunlight
that warms their backs,
beckoning them
to cross
the horizon
on tiptoe.

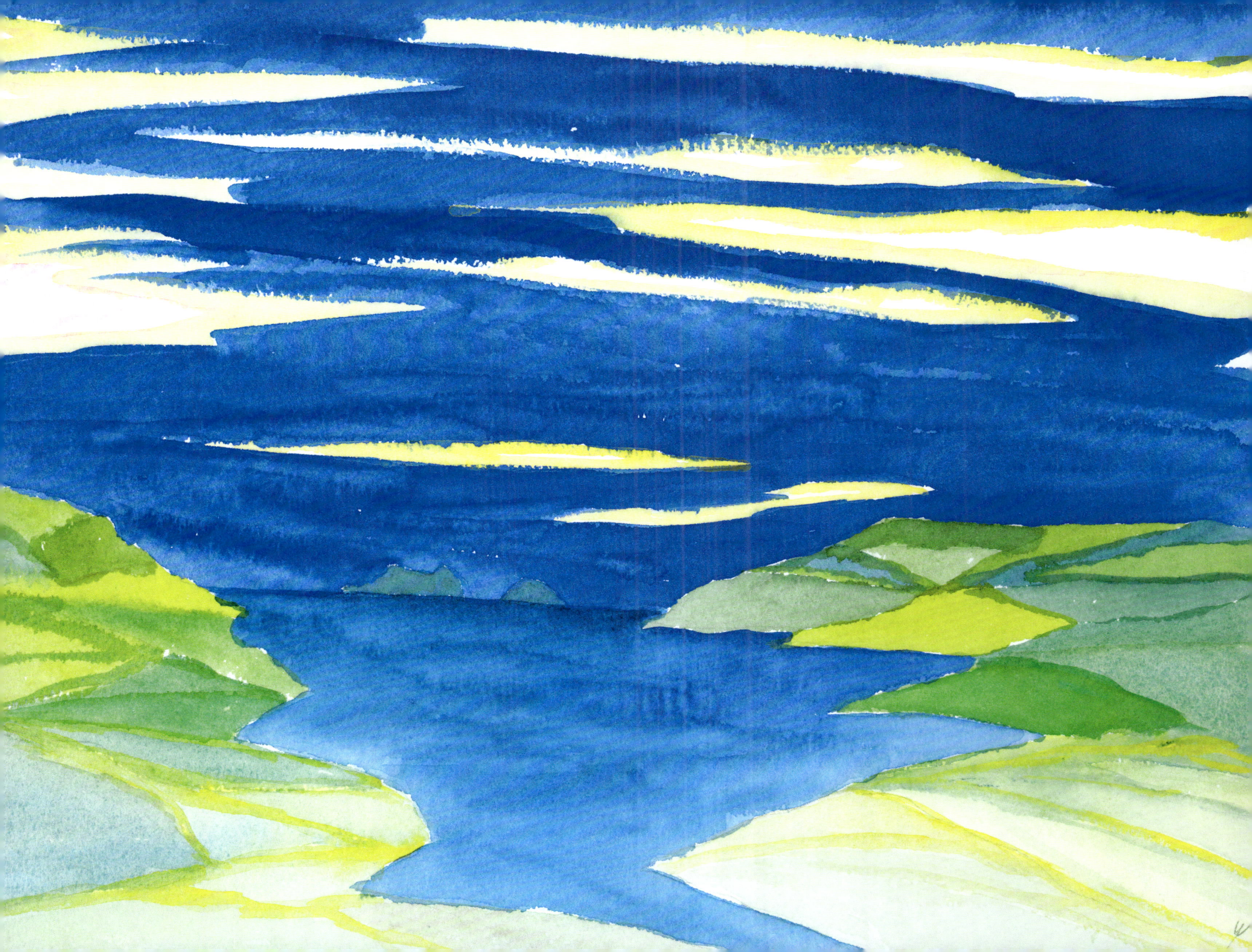

Telling All

An old woman
with silver hair
snorts
and shares
her "Harumph!,"
dismissing
the world's frivolity
and the tittering
of gossip –
gazing
at a middle-aged friend,
she tells her
that she has seen it all,
and that what matters
is dinner
served on time,
in a room
overlooking
a well-weeded
garden.

A Picky Dancing Partner

A calico cat
saunters
down the sidewalk,
flicking her tail,
as she zigzags
across cracks
in the pavement:
in no hurry
to waltz,
she scans
the jagged grass,
waiting
her turn
to foxtrot
with a blue jay.

Open Door Policy

An old house,
square-shouldered
and red-roofed
in its summer
white suit,
sets out
its front porch
to oversee
a green lawn's
growth,
while the portrait
of a saint
protects
its stately windows,
and a fence
of bright-eyed
flowers
naps,
beside a welcome mat
of bleary-eyed
sunlight.

Old Point Loma House

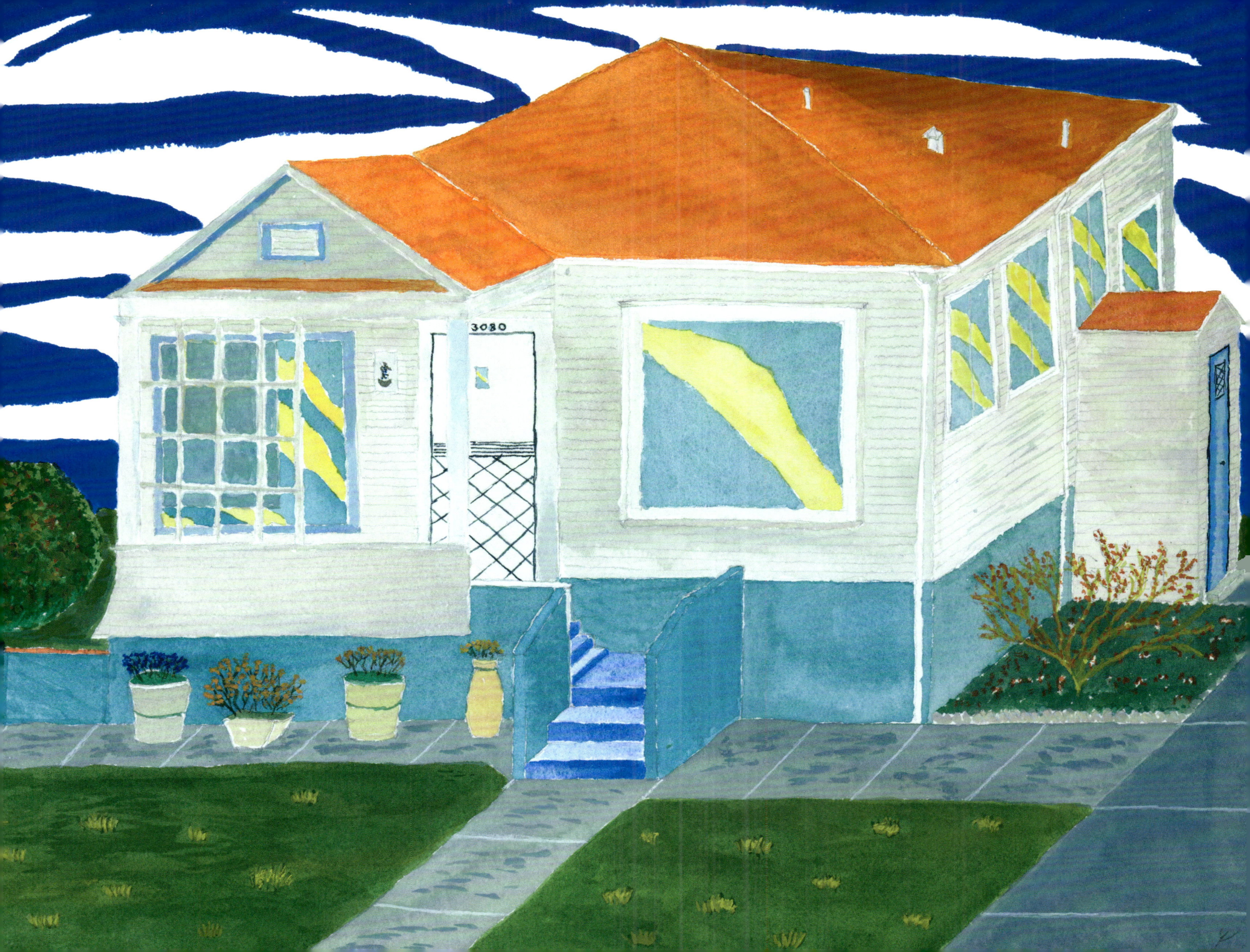
3080

A Long Engagement

The clear-eyed
ocean,
awakening
to a day
of untidy
sunlight,
winks
at more than one
lollygagging sailboat,
then settles down
to a day
of kindhearted
glances,
toward a shore
that welcomes
a vagabond's tall tales,
whether trumpeted
or whispered.

Coming True

The golden coast,
aglow
on a sunlit
morning,
stretches out
beside purple waves,
as the land
tumbles down
to the ocean,
where small boats
glide
across the calm water,
and a sky
with no limits
rises
above mountains
that lift their white crests
to a sun
that smiles at their ancient locks.

At Home

Mountains
look over the shoulder
of the sandy
coast,
then lift
their heads,
to catch sight
of a cloud
that has beached itself
on their smiling
brows.

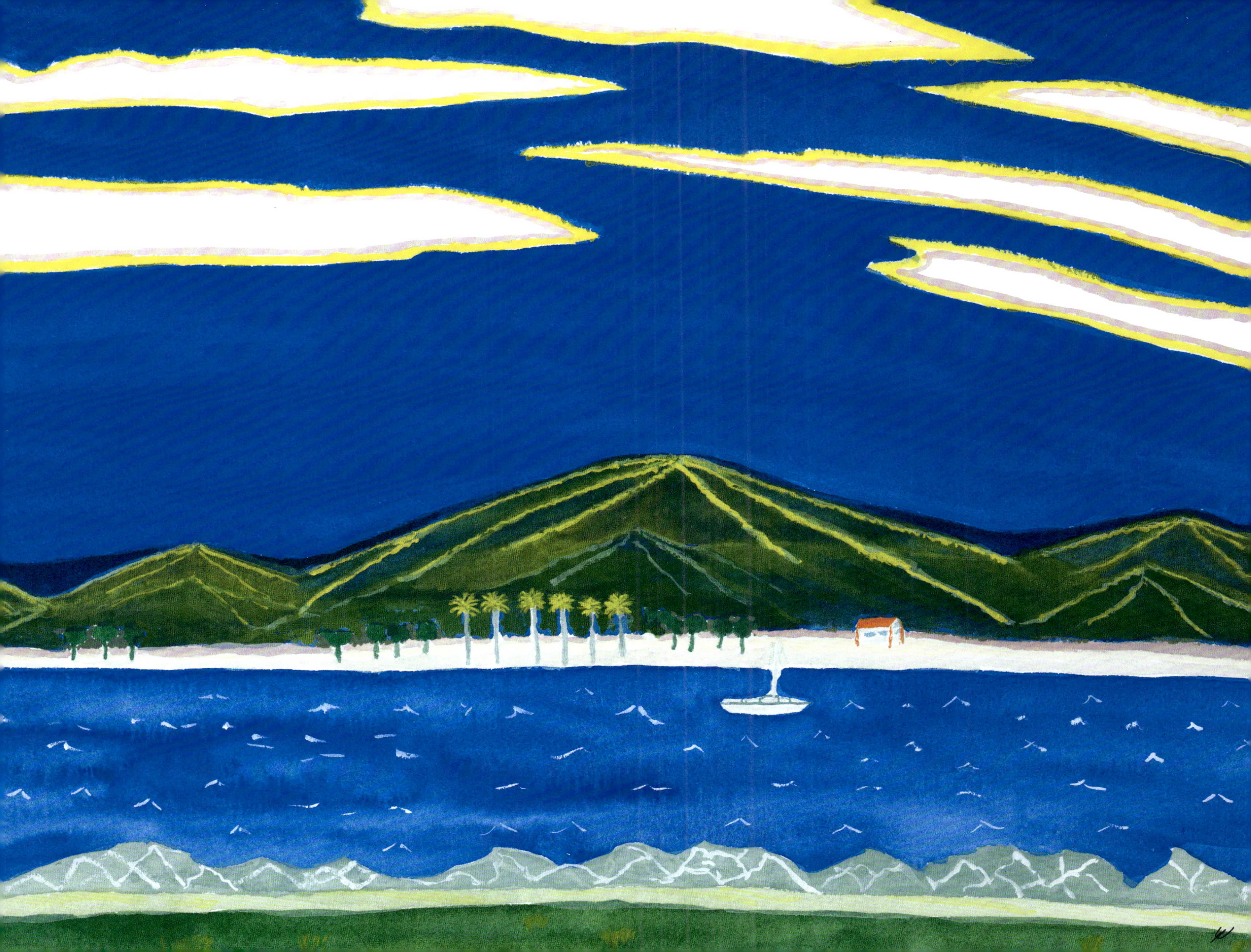

Winter Laughter

An old woman
hobbles forth,
from the car
to a flung-open
door –
she drops her purse,
then pulls off
her rain bonnet,
as her red hair
flares up,
in golden light
that waltzes
onto the sidewalk.

A Stitch in Time

An old friend
once told me
his rule:
on an airline flight,
never sit next
to a man
who is writing poetry;
if a fellow
starts that,
get up
and move;
of course,
he later
took up knitting,
to calm his frazzled nerves,
and enjoyed
the space
that an empty seat
next to him
afforded,
or the touch
of a grandmother's
all-knowing hand.

Living On

A gray bird,
fallen
on the stone-cluttered
pavement,
softens
the dark street
into a cloud,
while the wind
tugs
at its feathers,
and a spring tree
sends its shadows
to caress
a quiet
minstrel.

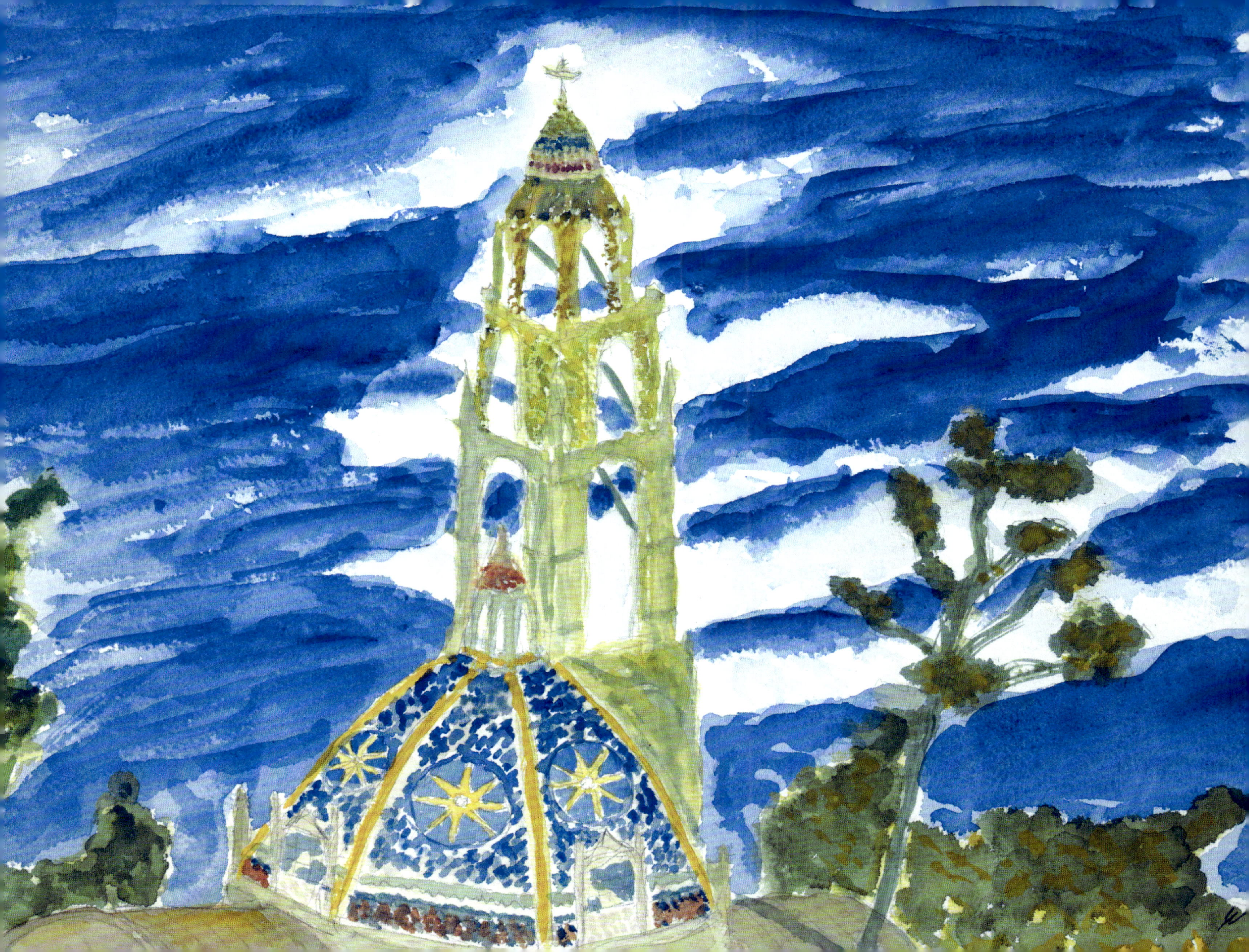

High Hopes

The stingy-fingered
crabapple tree,
with stubby gray knuckles
and gnarled branches,
blossoms
at last
on the cusp
of spring –
pink flowers
appear
on the tips
of twigs,
and the fists
of the old tree open up,
into children’s hands
offering
bouquets
to a blue sky.

Long Distance

Here,
in paradise,
the middle-aged man
is already
bound away,
having ventured
as far as he dares –
now he is spun
back,
even at the moment
that he sighs
and promises himself
that he will stay –
it is too late,
as a hibiscus blossom
in an exotic garden
droops,
and he hears
a dog bark
in Pittsburgh.

Wise to Flowers

An orange-slatted
botanical building,
with its high cupola
and outstretched wings,
invites
pavement-dwellers
to enter,
and to smell
a bold lily
in a cloistered
rainforest.

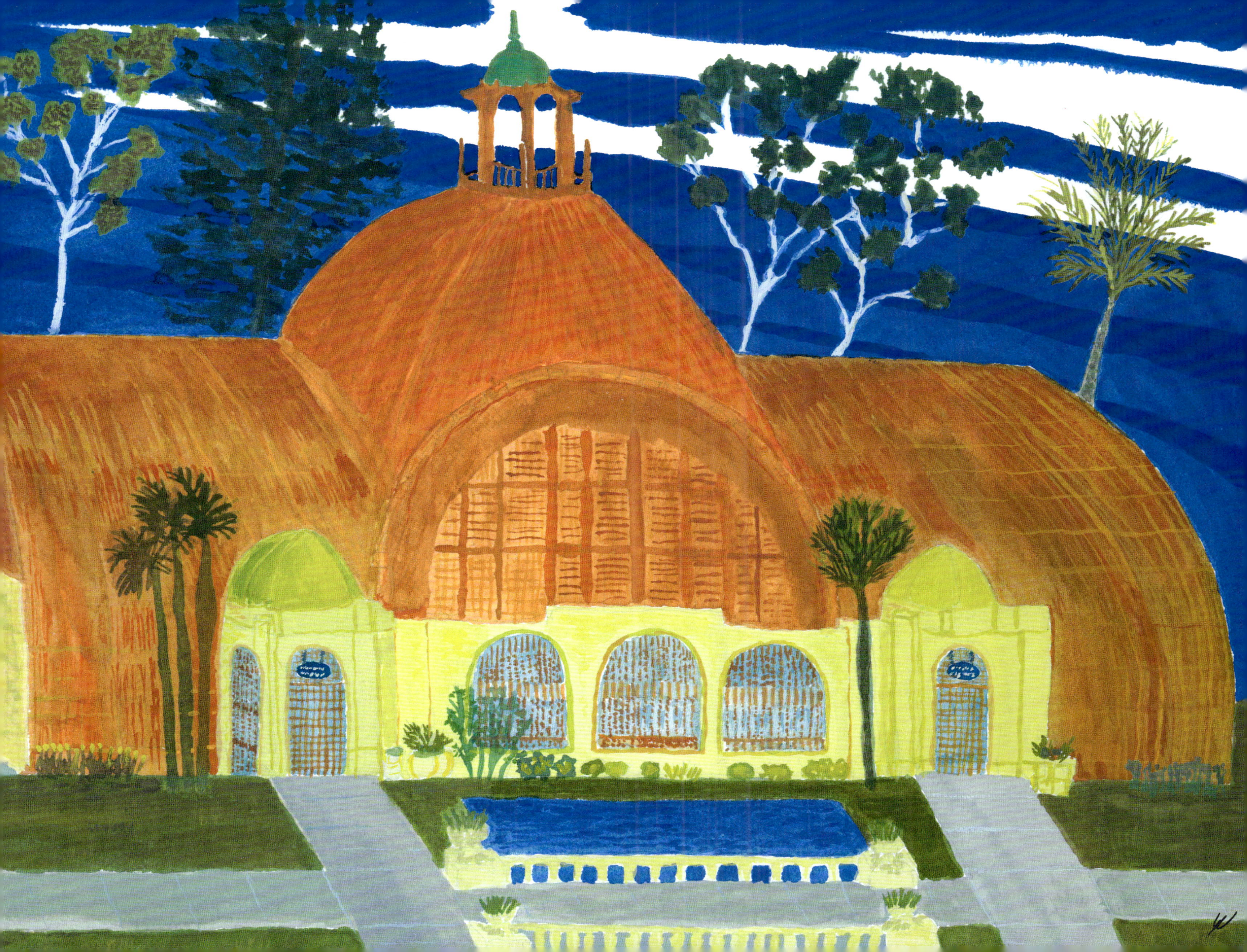

A Burger and Fries

A middle-aged man
sits
in an all-night
restaurant
at dusk,
eating his hamburger
alone –
gazing out
at the buildings that suddenly
illumine
their smiles,
he lets
the last
of the sun's
golden light
settle
about his shoulders,
keeping him company
at his table
for one,
high above a floor
that glistens
beneath a fluorescent
sky.

An Eye for Beauty

Pigeons
in the fog,
parading
on the rain-speckled sidewalks,
strut
and circle
and bob their heads,
and, pausing,
keep a lookout
for a wayward
crumb,
or a hand
that has no problem
with feeding
the beak
that pecks it.

At a corner,
a bird
looks both directions,
then snubs them both,
to flatter
a low-lying tree branch
in blossom.

Heading Home

A Golden Retriever
swims in the bay,
splashing his way
through the blue water,
as he splits open
the waves
as if they were
stands of grass,
then scampers
onto the shore,
to give his owner
a shower,
with a rainbow
thrown in
for luck,
while the sky
makes room for clouds
that dog-paddle
among calm shallows.

West Mission Bay

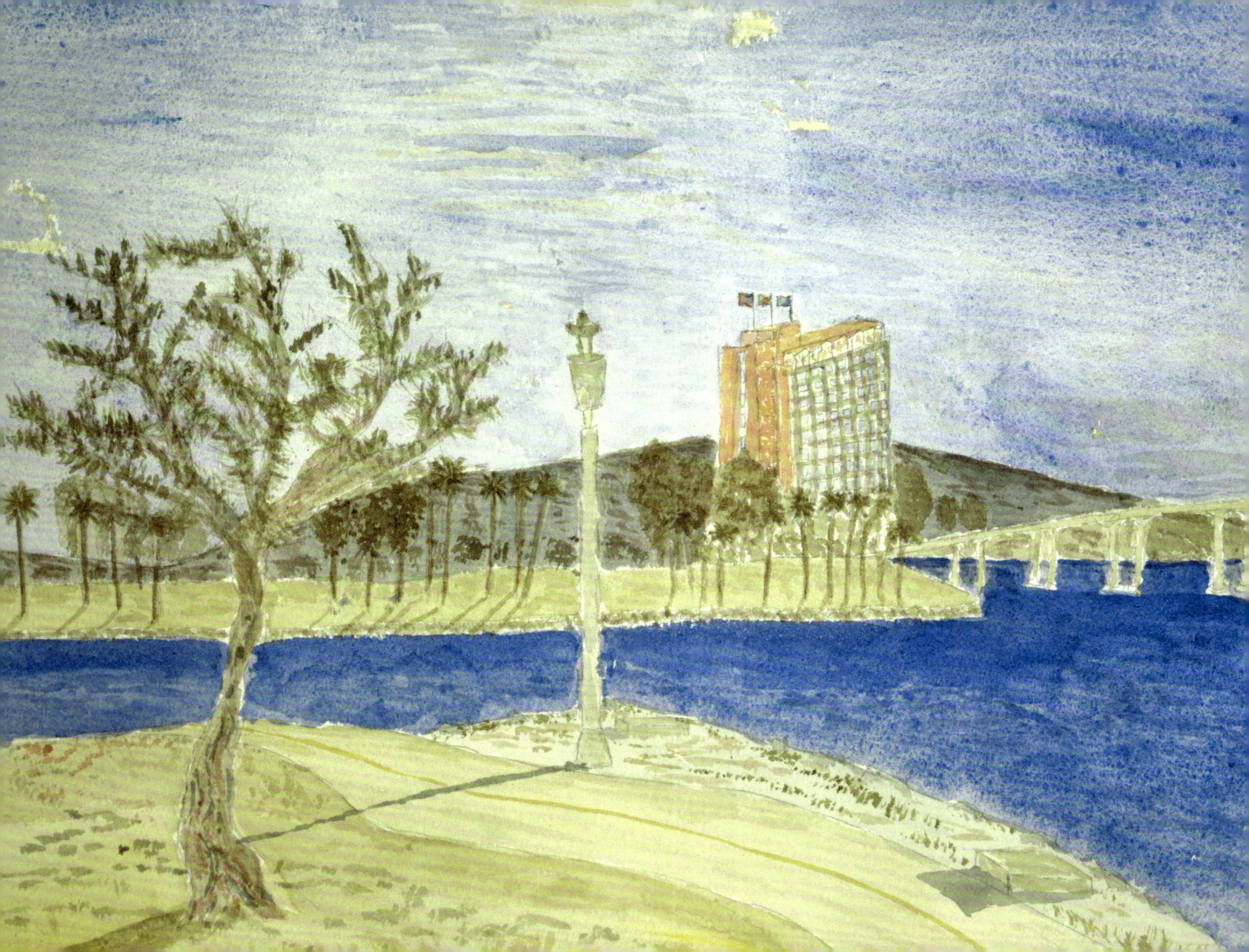

A Calm Harbor

A shadow
upon the ocean,
a floating
island
that swims
in the shade,
embraces
the surf
that combs out
its hair,
the beaches
that welcome
the caress
of its homecoming.

Coming Home

On a sunny day
in winter,
you sit
beside a window,
watching clouds
clot the sky,
and green hills
scramble down
to the ocean;
seeing no reason
to give up
on a quiet season,
you smile
at a road
that makes its way
out of a grove
of shadows,
into the warm palm
of a golden
valley.

A Wild-Eyed Fan

A bridge
and a mountain –
what more
could you ask for?

The ocean's
thrown in,
to applaud
two trapeze artists,
who both
rise above
their fear
of heights.

Coronado Bridge from Shelter Island

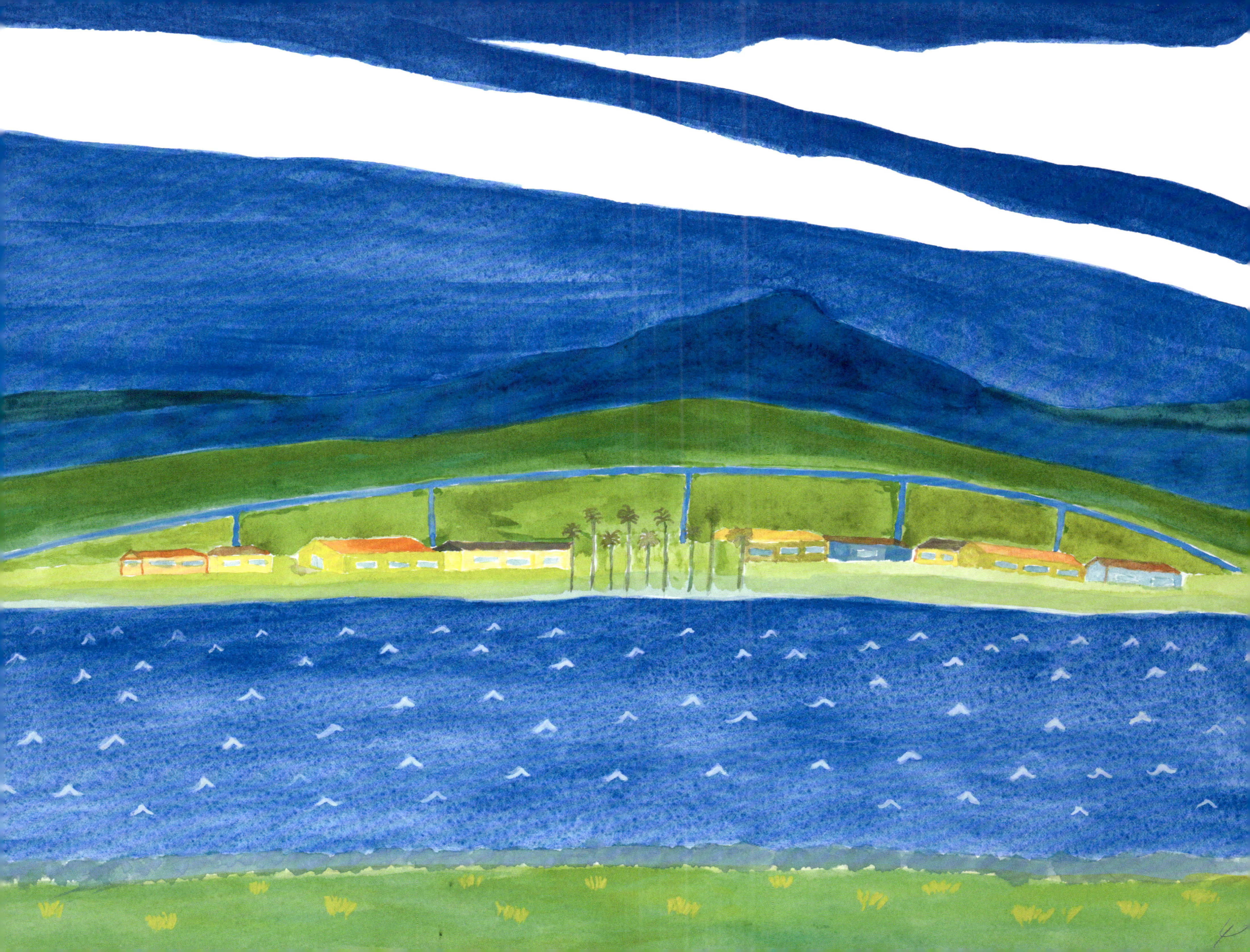

Finding Joy

The ocean,
always working,
inspires you
with its waves –
swimming skyward,
they never tire,
taking with them
boats
that love
to dance.

Starting Over

An old woman
with a multicolored
shawl
saunters
down a path,
scattering smiles
on an absentminded
afternoon,
when sunlight and shadows
play tag
with each other,
and the ocean
swims away
from the shore,
leaving behind
its embroidery of surf,
to embrace
ships
that kick up
their heels.

High Spirits

Whitecaps
under a cookie-cutter sky
flash
their messages
of high-flying
elation,
while the land
pieces together
a rainbow
mosaic,
and a solitary
sailboat
leaps
and takes wing,
to keep pace
with the wind
and the somersaulting
light.

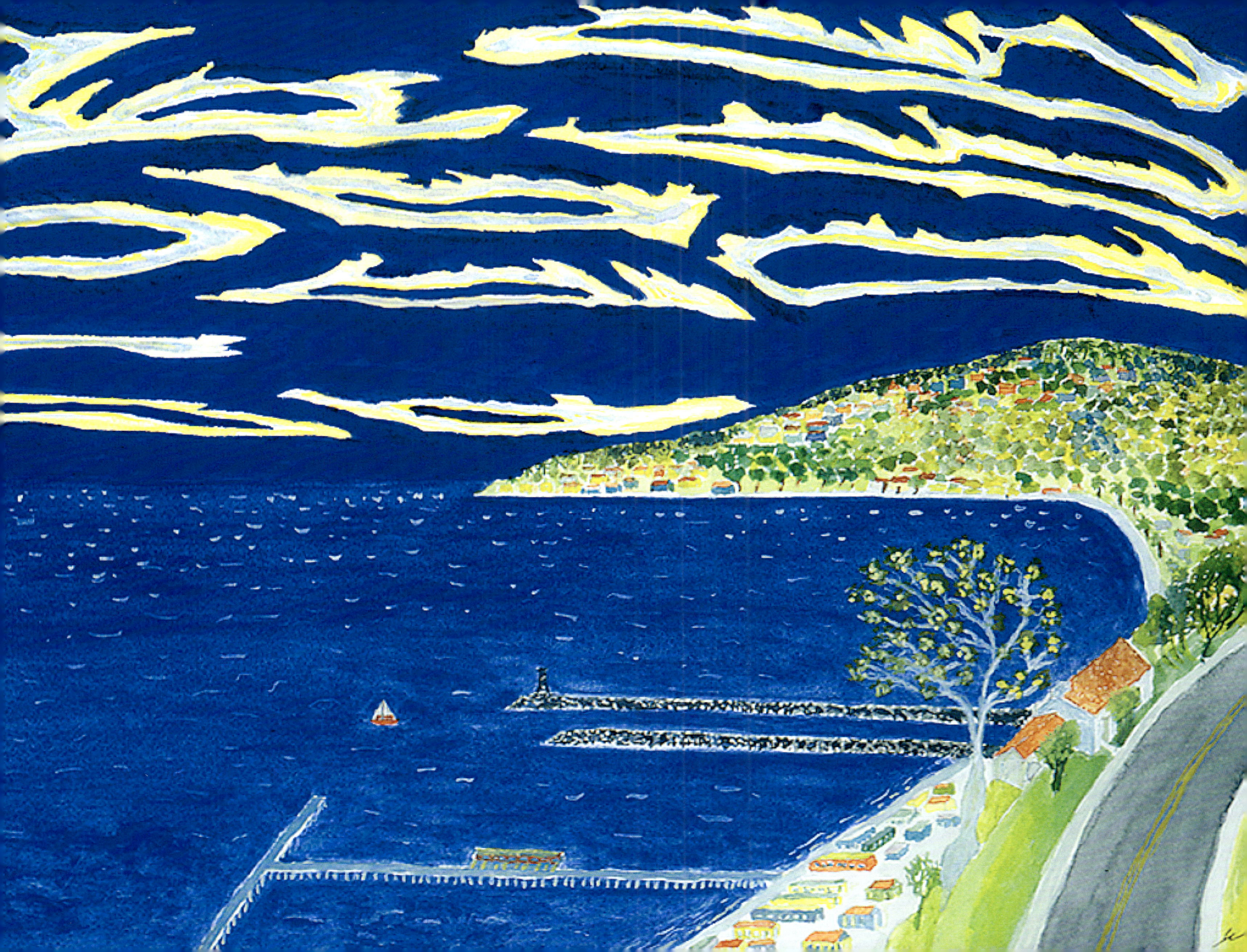

Celebration

Birds sing
at dawn,
serenading
an orchid sky,
and, heard
or unheard,
flutter up
out of boughs,
whose leaves
plant
a garden
of soft-eyed
shadows
that are
all ears.

Shooing Away Fog

The sky
clears
at last,
and the ocean
settles down,
under a gentle
blue coverlet
that was made
for an autumn
nap.

Finding His Way

An old man
trundles
down the street
to the coast,
to a park
where the ocean
tugs and laughs
at the beach,
which whispers
in reply
its constant farewell,
its lament
for palm trees
that sigh
at soft breezes
that are just
passing through.

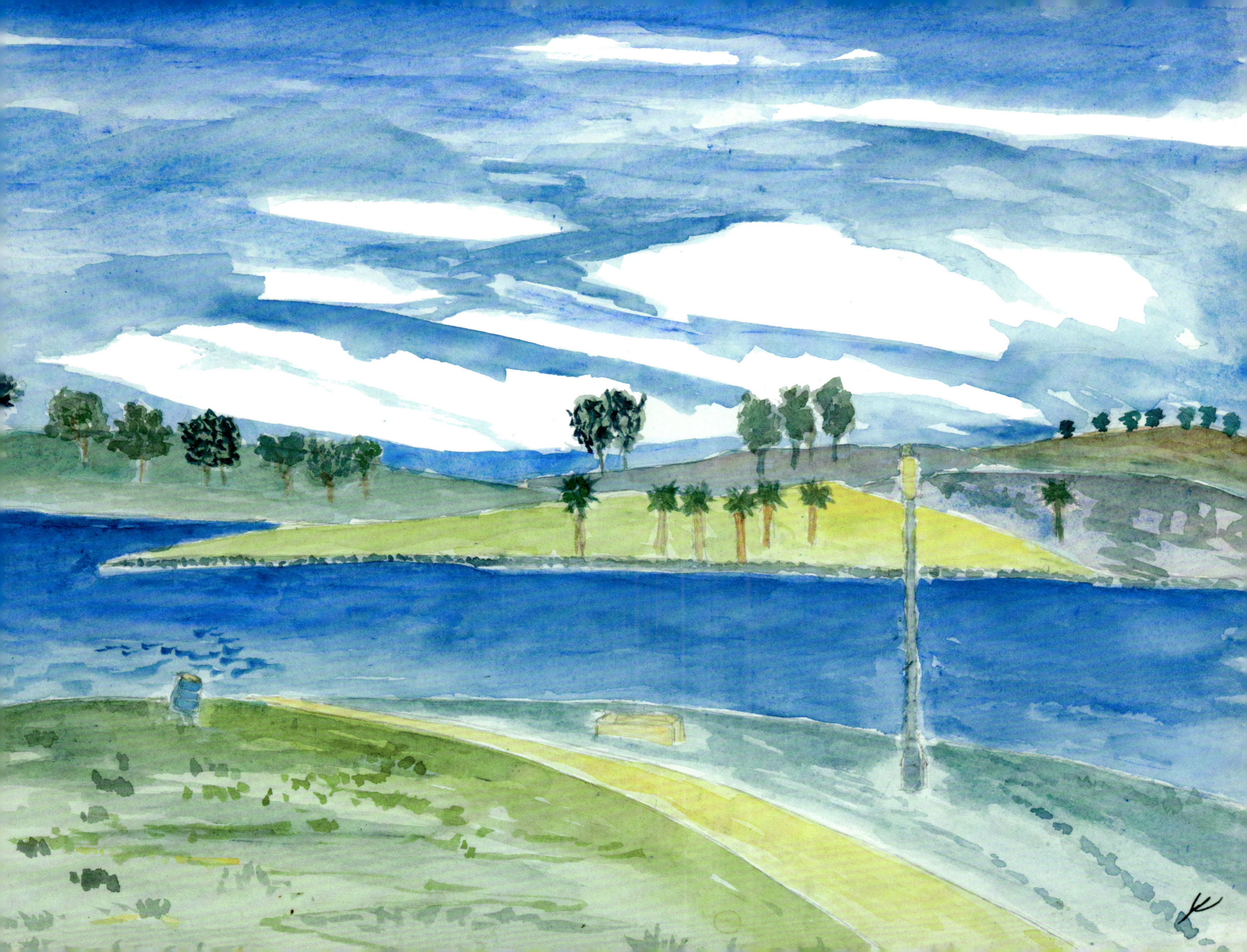

Greeting the Sun

Painting
a red-lettered sign
on a bright day
in October,
you let
the orange sunlight
divide
the letters
with its soft-hued
fingerprints,
all of them
holding
the words
together,
with a smile
as eloquent
as the first
blush
of a baby-faced
rose.

A Homecoming

A young man
gazes
at photos
of his daughter,
smiling
as she beams at him,
while he waits
for the sky
to clear –
her eyes
are her mom's,
and he welcomes
their gentleness,
while the photos
guard their secrets,
and the young father
daydreams
of laughter.

A Winter Marriage

Stars
reel and tumble
all night long,
until, at first light,
the gray chalkboard
of the sky
is wiped clean,
and the light,
overflowing,
unfurls,
from the land
to the ocean,
a band
of blue and gold,
which floats
to the top
of the sky,
before settling down
with the horizon.

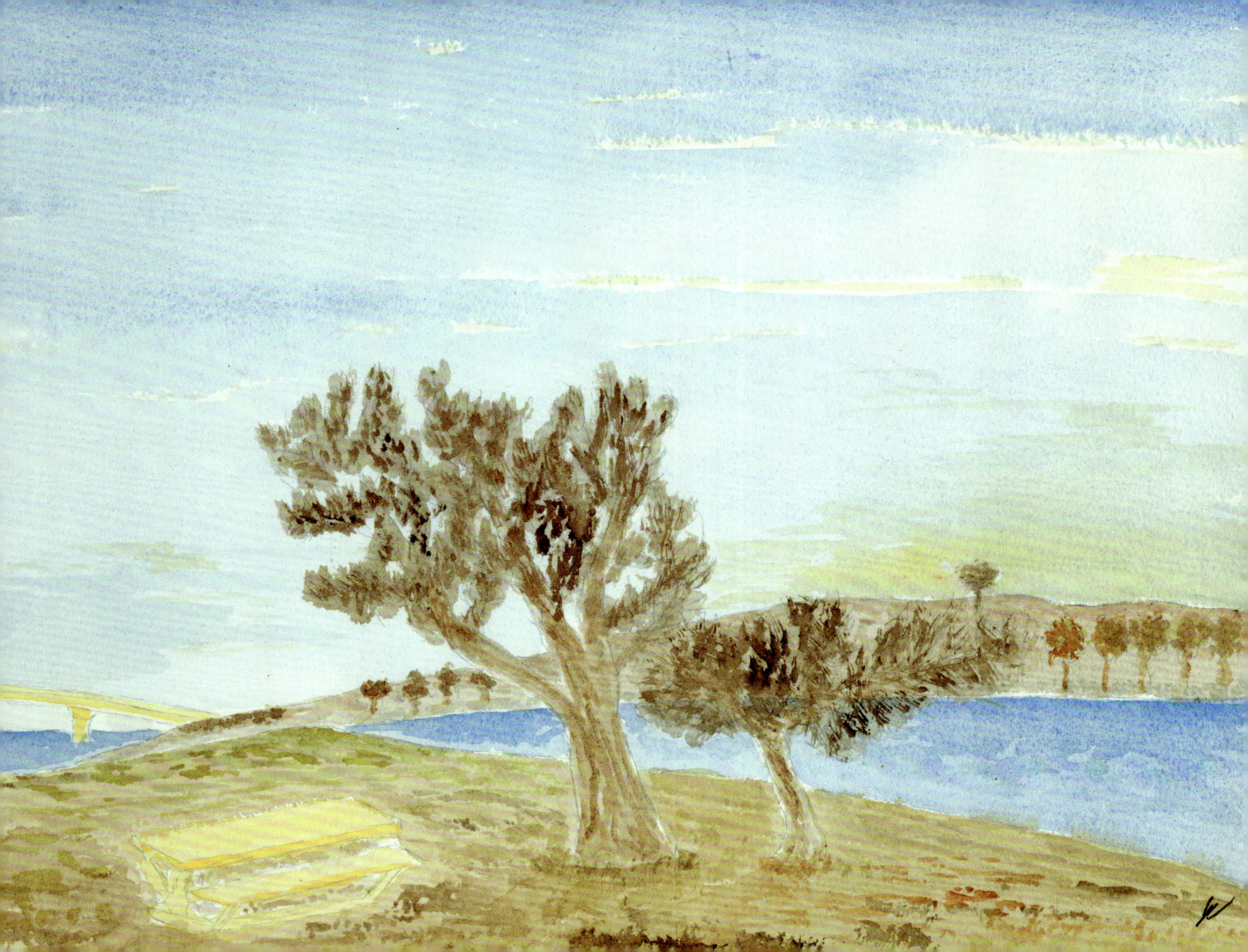

Get Up and Go

Running
among shadows
and sunlight,
you swerve
and zigzag,
and, finally
finding
your stride,
leap
into the air,
to give your feet
a toehold
in the sky.

Glimpsing a Lei

An old man,
toddling forth
at dawn,
glances
at the ocean,
at the topsy-turvy
waves,
and does not feel
abandoned
in the silver-haired fog,
for beyond it,
a bouquet
of sunlight
stands ready
to wash
ashore.

Beyond the Darkness

Coming home
in lingering
light,
with only the stars
for company,
you gaze out
at the last
of the light,
and, smiling,
catch sight
of cities
festooned
with streetlamps,
and a horizon
so golden
that you cannot imagine
a brighter road
home.

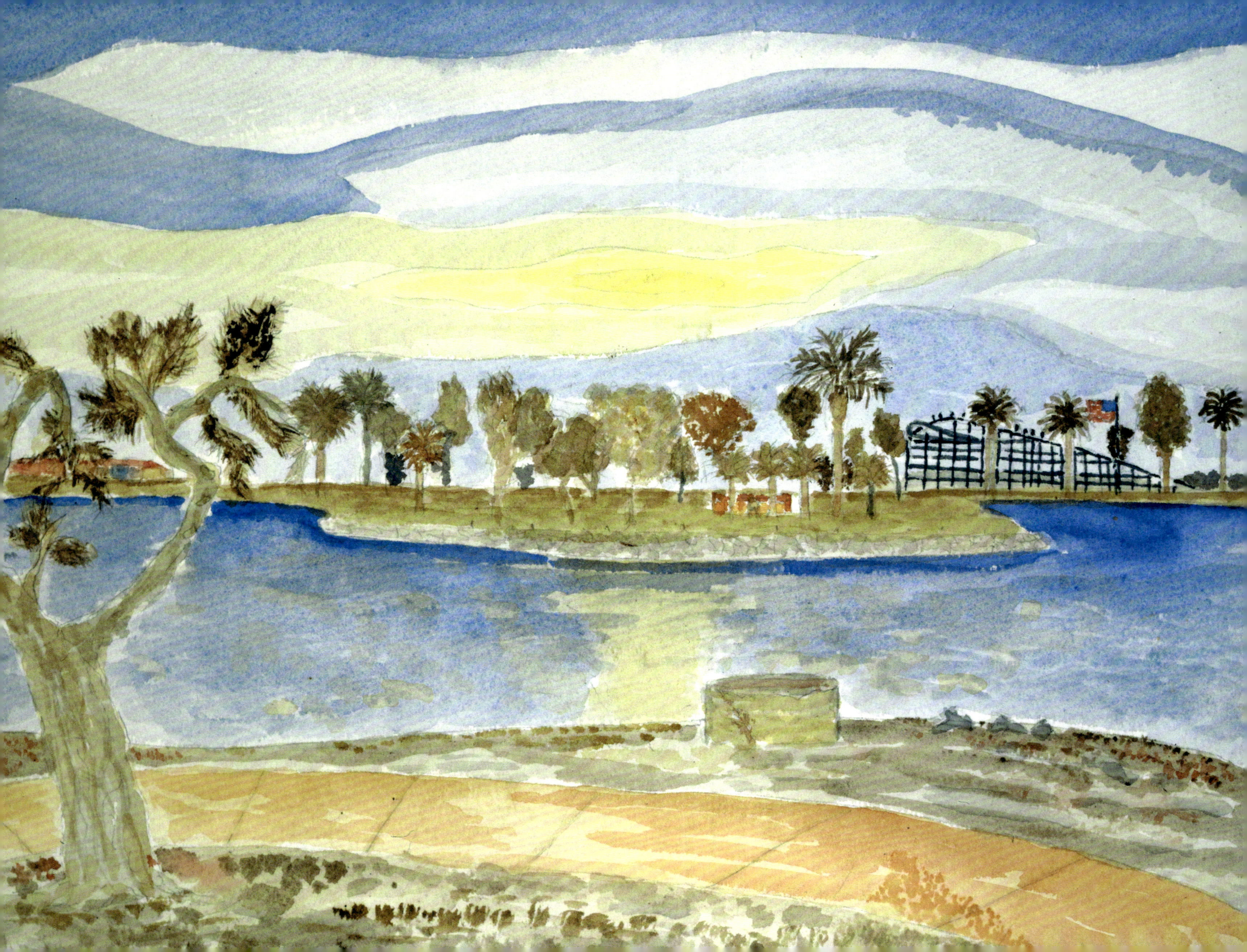

Rewriting Geography

The city,
bathed in sunlight,
tumbles
down to the bay –
dipping its fingertips
in the turquoise water,
it flings
rainbow confetti
into the high plains
of the sky.

Beyond Hard Knocks

After a night
of hard drinking,
the womp-womp lady,
wealthy
and high-heeled,
shows up
in the supermarket's
express checkout line,
where she buys
gourmet coffee
and a weight-loss
concoction –
with her straw hat
and blue jeans
and bright-flowered
shirt,
she could pass
for Ava Gardner,
long after her prime –
and still
her eye makeup
sparkles,
and her scarlet nails
flash,
as she asks
the young checker
how much cash
she can get back;
and when he answers $100,
she takes her time,
toying with her bank cards,
as she glances
back
at the five gawkers
who sure as shooting
can wait in line,
for the privilege
of watching her
sashay
away,
on what she knows
will be
a very good day.

A Long Honeymoon

The city
and the harbor,
married
at twilight,
smile
at one another,
content
to share
a breeze
tinged
with laughter.

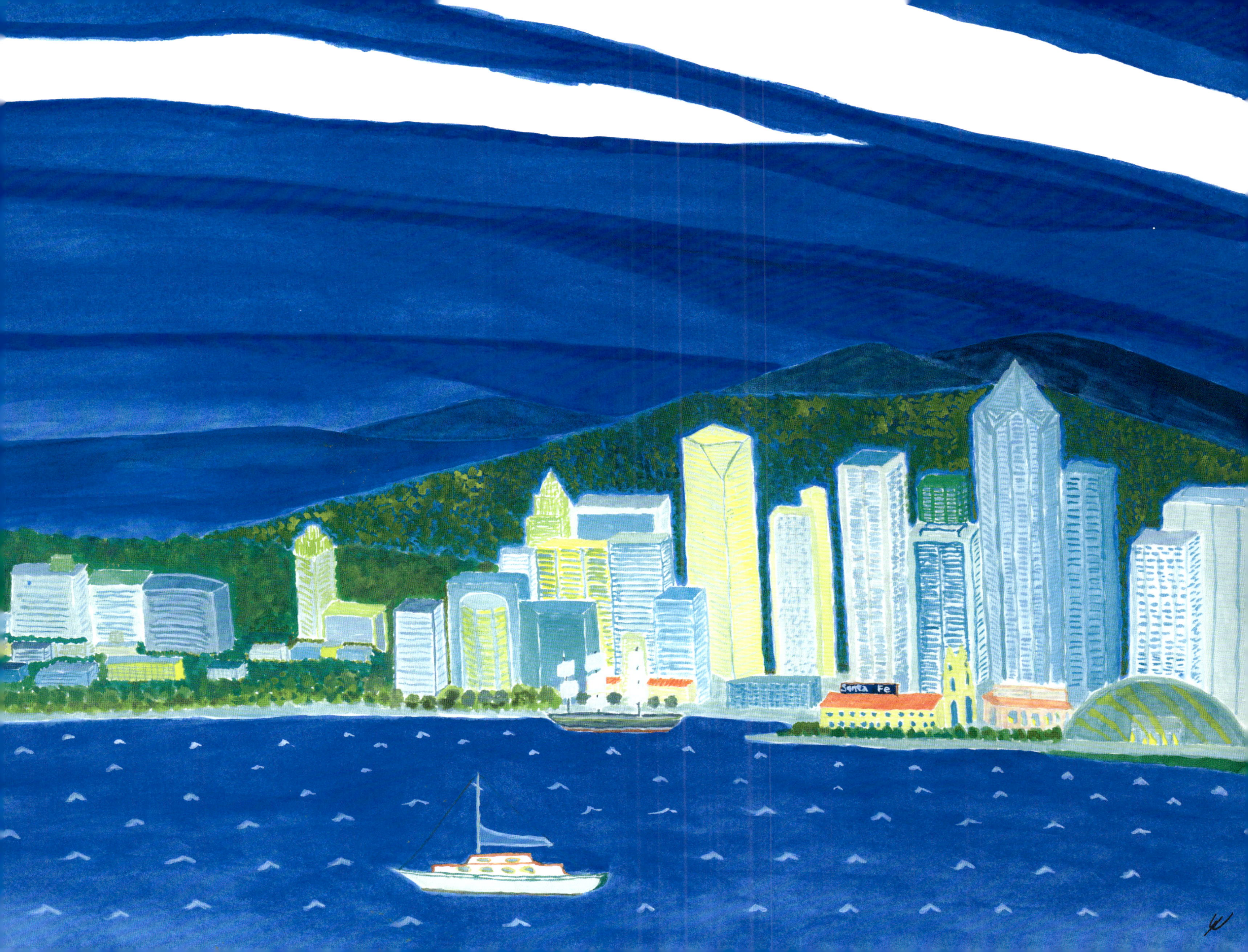
Santa Fe

An American Life

When I was young,
I never knew
how important
Chevrolets were,
in the greatest
scheme of things –
how they could preside
over weddings
and funerals,
or whisk people
across the dusty prairie,
or open their windshields wide
to everyone's
constellations.

Today
I appreciate
the thud
of steel doors,
the glint of chrome,
the guffaws
of tires,
but then,
when I should have known
what chauffeured people
past eternity,
I didn't understand
why Henry Ford
loved
rough-and-tumble
competition.

Breaking Bread

Two old women
in the supermarket
fuss
over loaves of bread,
not coarse-grained enough
for one,
too gritty
for the other,
until, shaking their heads,
they take
each other's hands,
and stroll
out of the sharp-tongued
bakery aisle.

Hoisting Anchor

An old naval base,
deserted now
to weeds,
offers its secret beauties
to wanderers
who crisscross it
daily –
watching the yellow buildings,
with their red-tiled rooves
and blue-framed windows,
stand up
to a fleet
of gray clouds,
you overhear
two birds
in a tree
sing,
as if the sky
were an open-armed
ocean.

Naval Training Center, Building 30

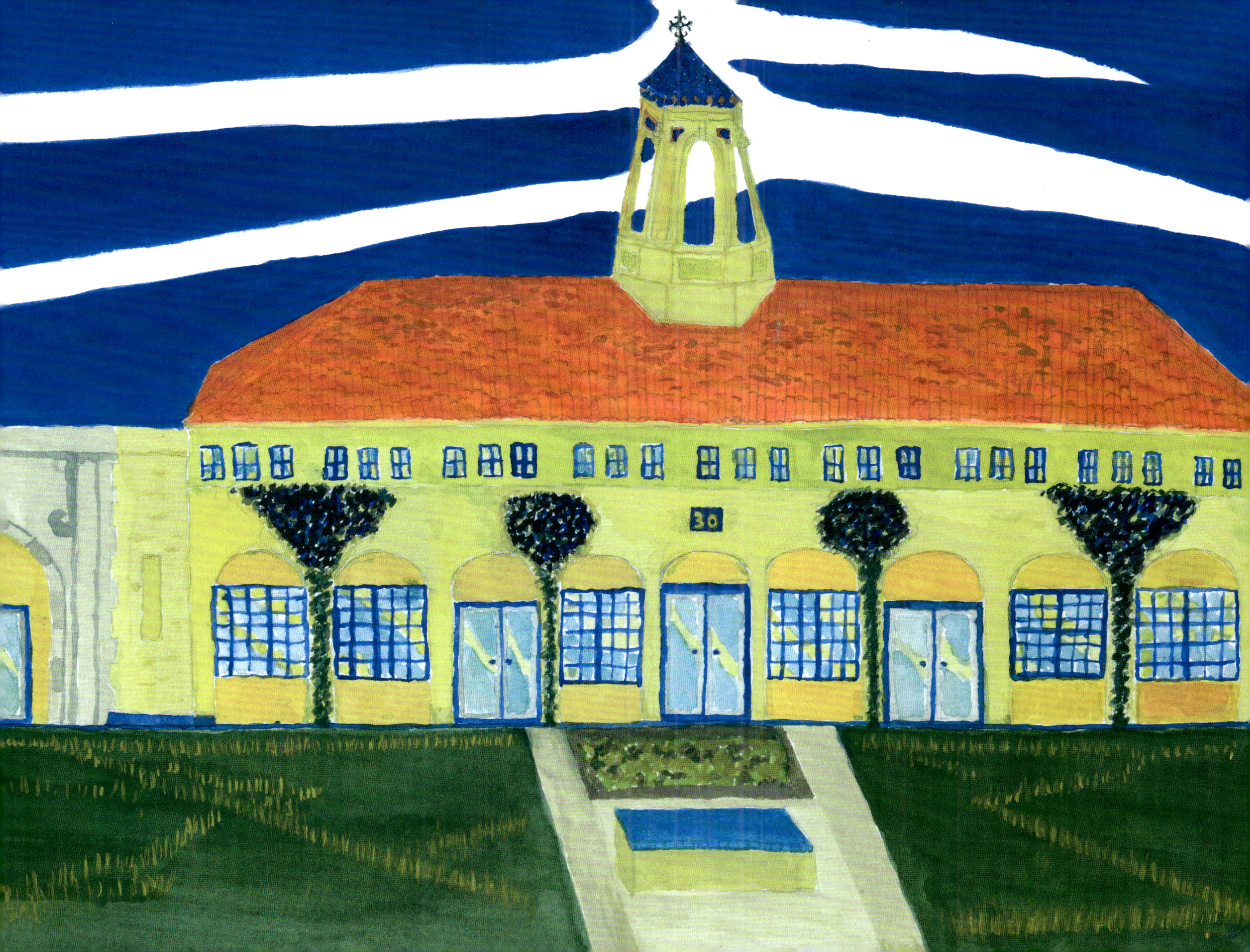
30

Buried Treasure

Gray pelicans,
diving
again and again
into the sunlight-lined
waves,
force them
to cough up
a school
of silver fish,
a pocketful
of dimes
with scales
as soft
as moonlight.

Looking Up

On the other side
of the canyon
stands
a jumble
of houses,
among which
an old cottage
holds its own
in the morning fog –
white-shingled,
with its gabled roof,
it sits proudly
on a corner lot,
with two black lawn chairs
guarding
its front lawn,
and a jacaranda tree
lending shade
to its green-shuttered
windows,
after all of the tree's
yellow blossoms
have fallen,
while the sky
opens a door,
to reveal a far rooftop
of ruby-lipped
tiles.

Old Friends

The ocean
paws
at the beach,
running
its fingertips
through the whispering
sand,
and then
settles down,
to chat
with the rocks,
which enjoy
now and again
a good slap
on the back.

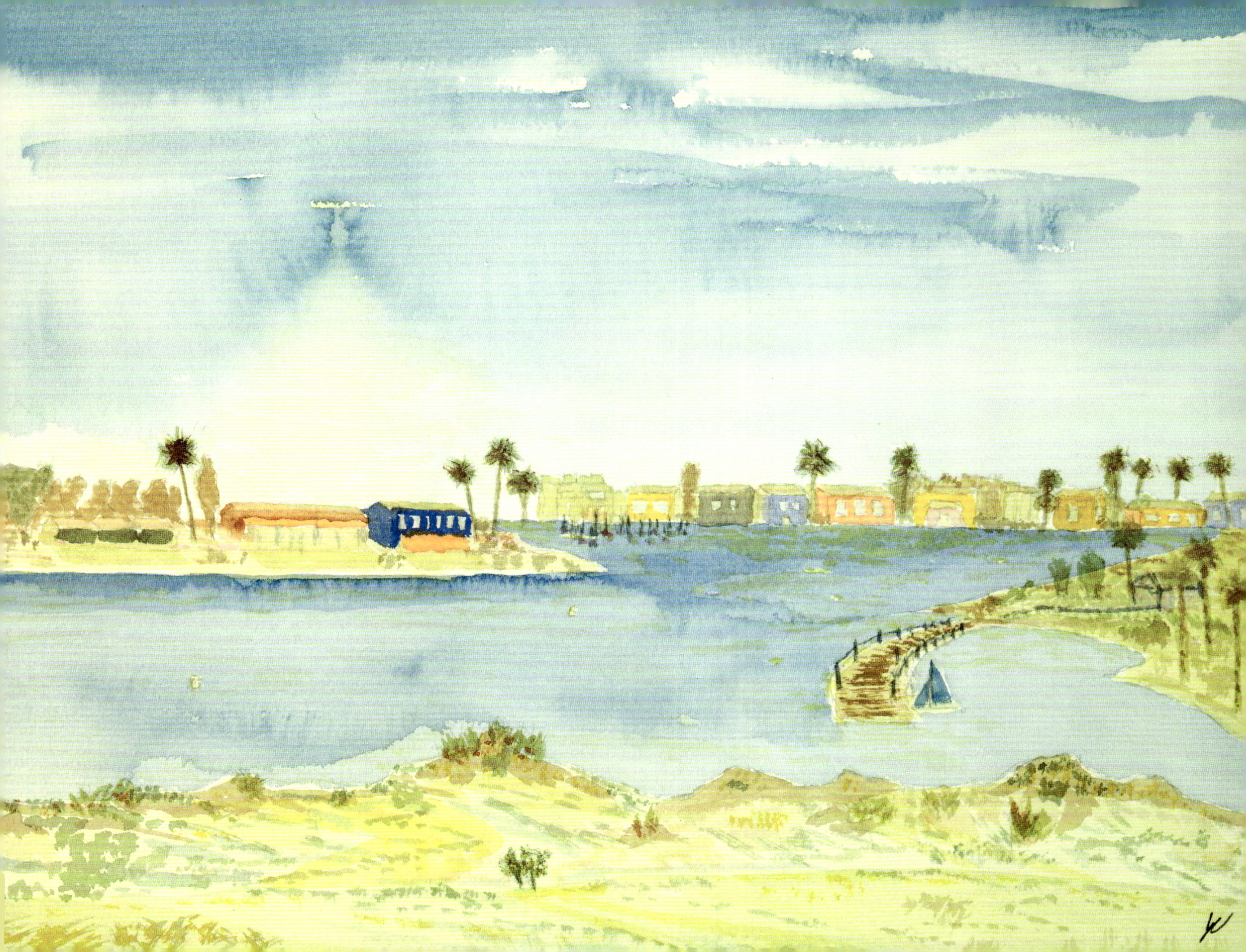

A Home Port

The ever-westering
sun,
journeying
toward Japan,
leaves behind
a fleet of clouds,
which, becalmed
at the horizon,
beam
in lingering
light.

Old Lovers

Dusk,
creeping
over
the land,
softens
its shirts
into folds,
pleats,
and wrinkles,
comfortable
old clothes,
to be worn
when courting
kind night,
with its elegant
gown
and its dime-store
diamonds.

Returning at Dusk

The sky,
all orange fire
and purple
embers,
settles down
to warm
the winter land –
a promontory,
an island,
a deep green
hillside
open their arms
to a flash
of light
beyond the horizon,
a golden
afterthought
of the licorice
ocean.

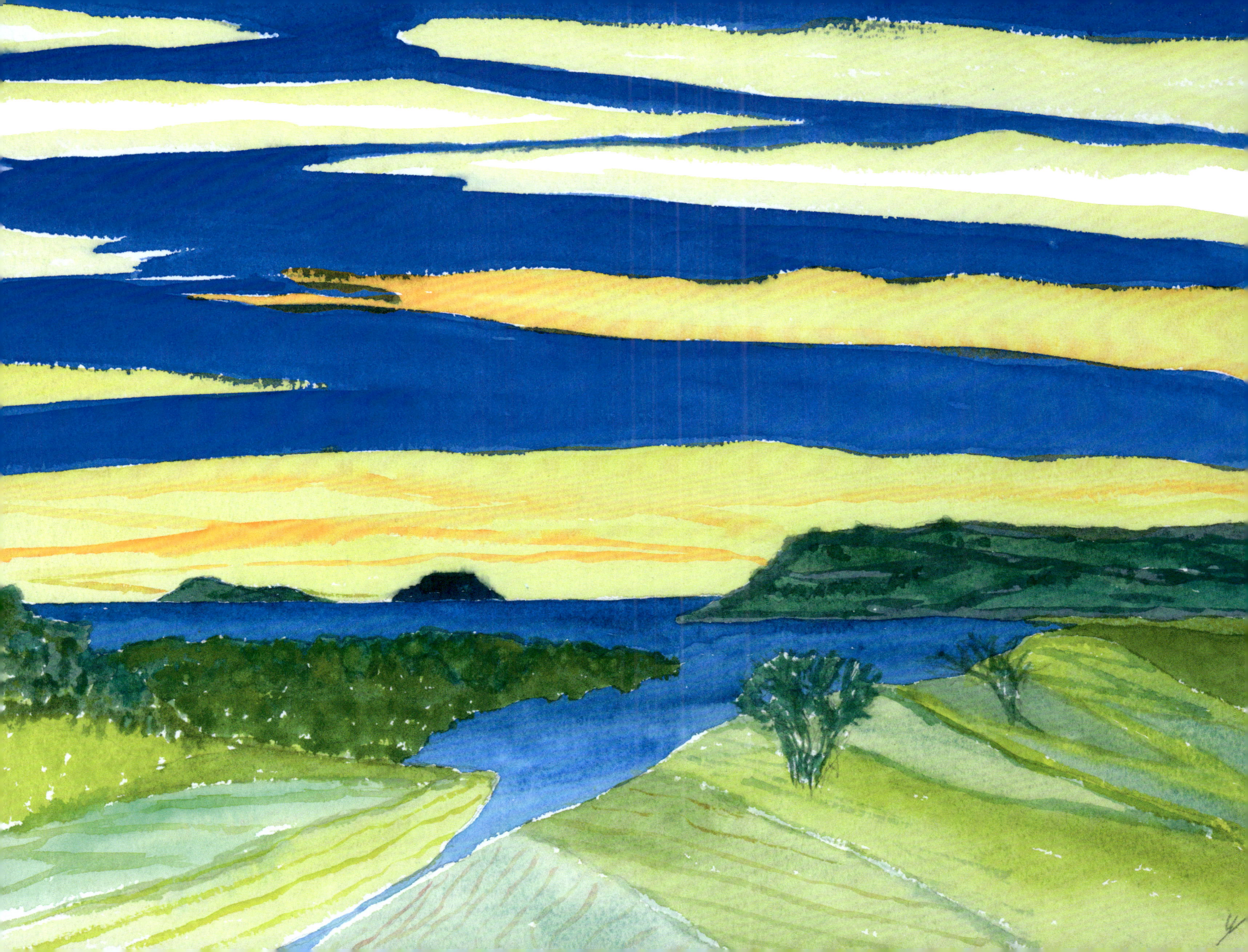

Spring Fever

Above the river,
hills
promenade,
keeping watch
for the western horizon
on parade,
and when the forests
and the fence
have slipped
out of sight,
the river
remains,
entangling itself
in a thicket
of far-flung
thunderheads.

Second Chances

Today
I rescued
a wasp
from a window
in my garage,
where he was seeking
light,
and found only glassy-eyed
hardness –
instead
of crushing him,
I coaxed him
out of doors,
where he repaid me
with a flight
as graceful
as that
of an angel,
into a blue sky
that neither of us
expected.

Finding Romance

A sailboat,
bobbing
at anchor
at dusk,
wallows
in golden light,
as its prow
faces out to sea
and its mast
points out
a bold star;
and still
it lingers,
to dance
with its purple
shadow,
which has waited
all day
to be thought
light
on its feet.

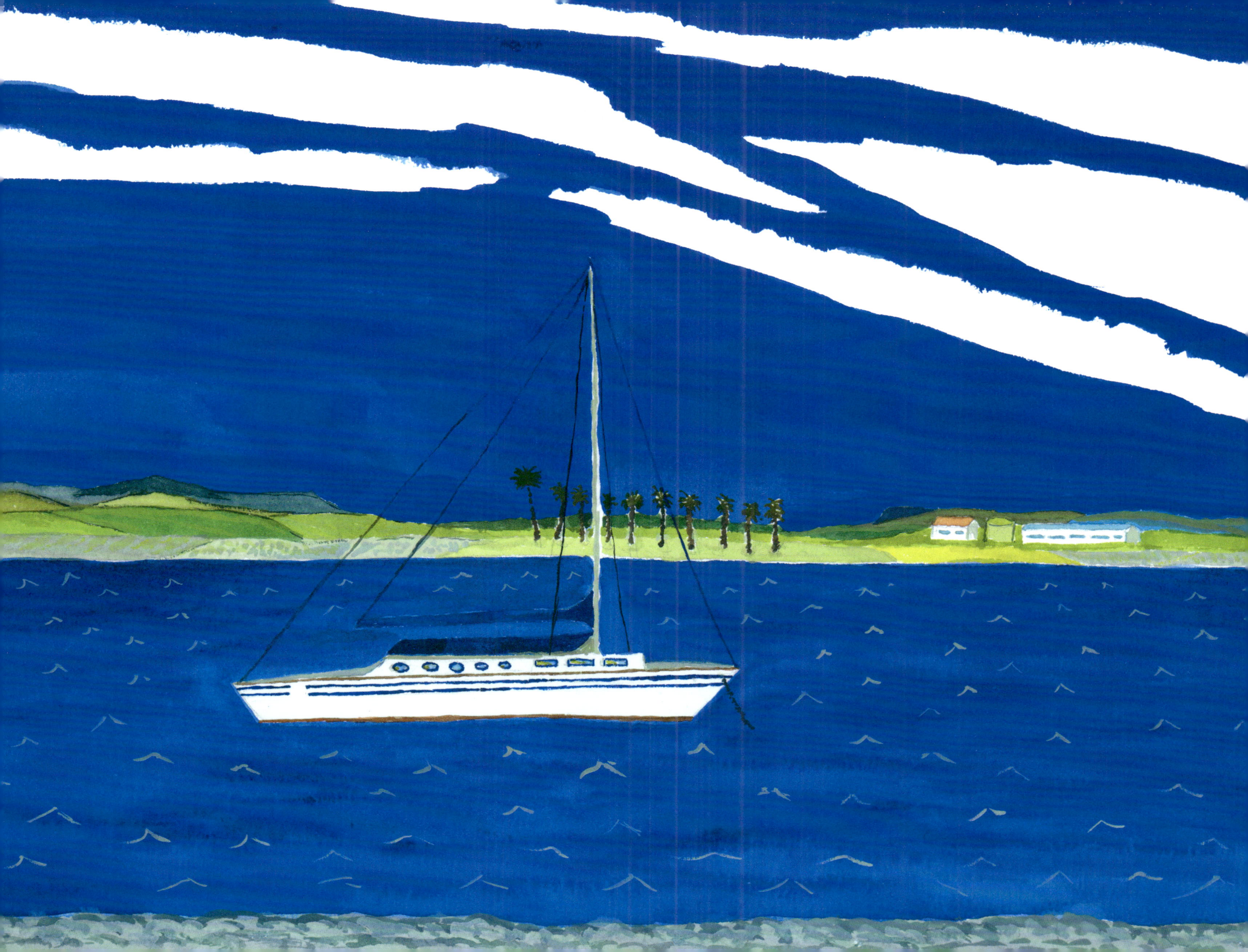

An Elegant Suitor

The wind
has combed out
the ocean,
for as far
as the eye can see,
and lent it
white locks,
to honor
its age,
and give it
a dapper
way home.

Among Friends

Great clouds
dot the sky,
raising their snowy
foreheads
to sunlight
that smiles
at bald-pated
giants.

Setting Out

Three palm trees
lean into the wind,
while their shadows
stretch out
toward the ocean –
intrepid voyagers,
they wave
to the horizon
and beyond it,
to a sun
that is always seeking
new masts
that may blossom
into islands.

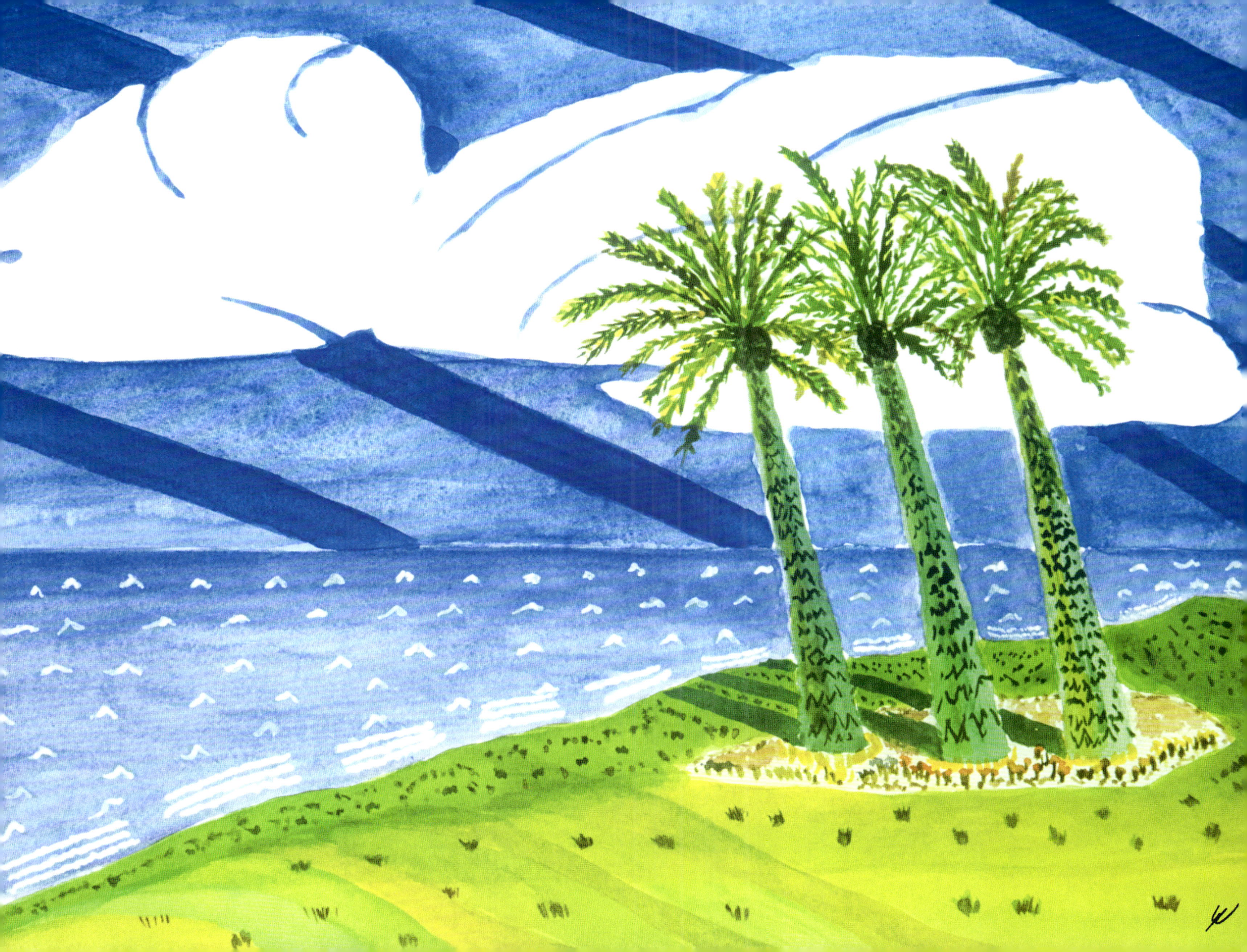

A Family Recipe

A pinch
of rain,
a dash
of sunlight,
and all that appears
is a tunnel
of blue sky
built
under a rainbow.

Our Daily Bread

A poem for everyone,
a word in each ear,
an echo
that answers
the silent –
give away samples
before it's too late –
your rainbow clothes
are tailored for strangers.

Between Squalls

Rain
along the coast,
a soft-spoken
temptress,
whispers
behind veils
of fog,
only to throw
caution
to the wind,
and rattle on
in a burst of sunlight
about something
as silent
as a wayfaring
rainbow.

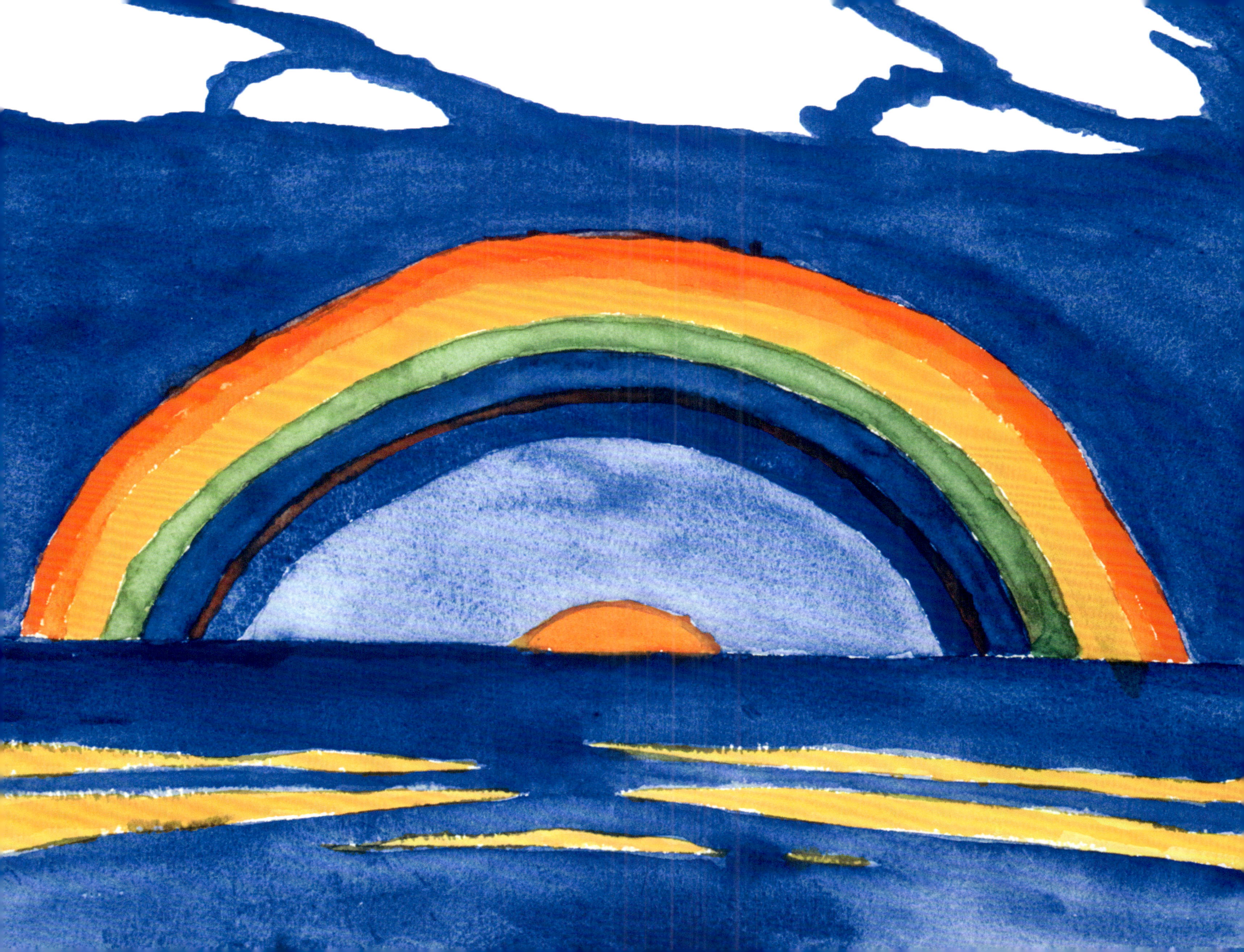

February Awakenings

Birds
sing out
at dawn –
LOUD,
to hasten
spring –
chirping
and trilling
and warbling
and twittering,
they greet
the timid
light,
with its gray eyes
and pale
complexion,
and its smile
that warms
to music.

A Year Later

A woman
of other times
raises her arms
in your dream
of a party,
and laughs
at the sight
of old friends –
light
floods the room,
and the windows
beam
light,
at the sight
of a redhead
who knew
that life
was the best joke
of all.

A Weekly Reflection

An old club,
named for calm Thursday,
sits
overlooking the ocean,
and, catching sight
of the glint
in waves' eyes,
flings open
its doors
to weary strangers,
delighted to dance
from
Friday
through Wednesday.

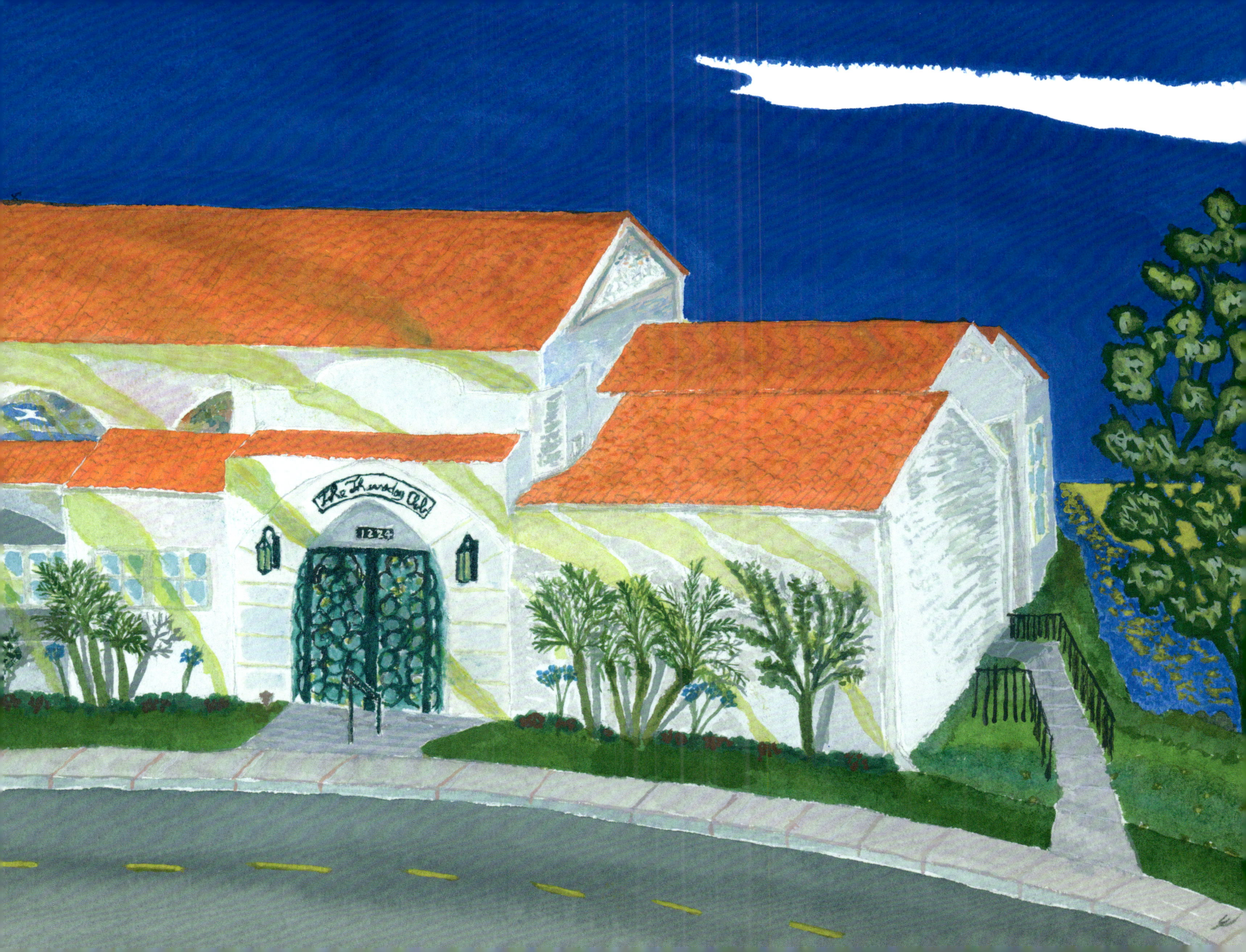
The Thursday Club
1224

Friendly Voyagers

Clouds
lead their shadows
across the ocean,
steering them
like islands
among the waves,
while sunlight
brightens
a road
to the horizon,
a thoroughfare
that has never
lost its way.

Without a Frame

Golden haze
above the coast
softens
the sky
into a fresco,
a painting
of a light-crowned
ocean,
a portrait
of a smiling
Venus.

Bedding Down

The western sky,
clearing
at sunset,
lets late light
escape
through its fingers,
then smiles
at softhearted
clouds
that settle
for the horizon's
unpadded
shoulder,
finding it
pillow enough
to make them
forget
all
except the wide-eyed
stars.

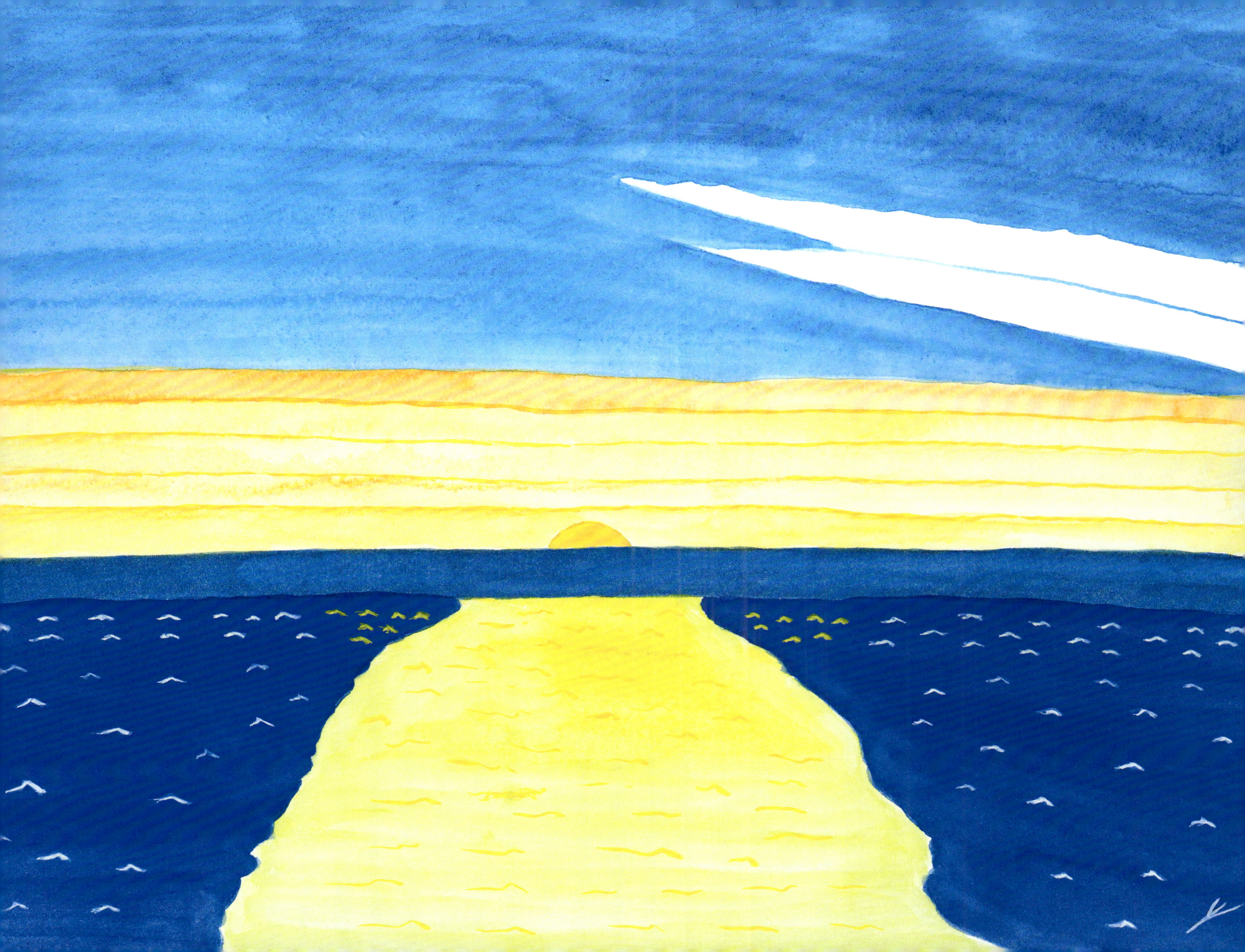

The Other Side

A middle-aged guy
with greasy, gray-streaked hair
and a wild-eyed
Hawaiian shirt
ambles
down the street,
with a hot brunette
on his arm;
headed
for the harbor,
he swaggers past the train tracks,
with a grin
on his face
and no regrets
about having
gotten lost.

The Right Station

An old man
in a brown suit
falls asleep
on the train,
as his chin
drops
onto his chest,
and his tie
lolls
across his yellow shirt –
awakening,
he glances up
at his dour
compartment companions,
his eyebrows
signaling his intention
to disembark
at the next
friendly
bar.

Points East

An old
railroad depot,
beaming
at strangers,
raises
its towers
like golden torches,
lit by mountains
and train tracks
from Santa Fe.

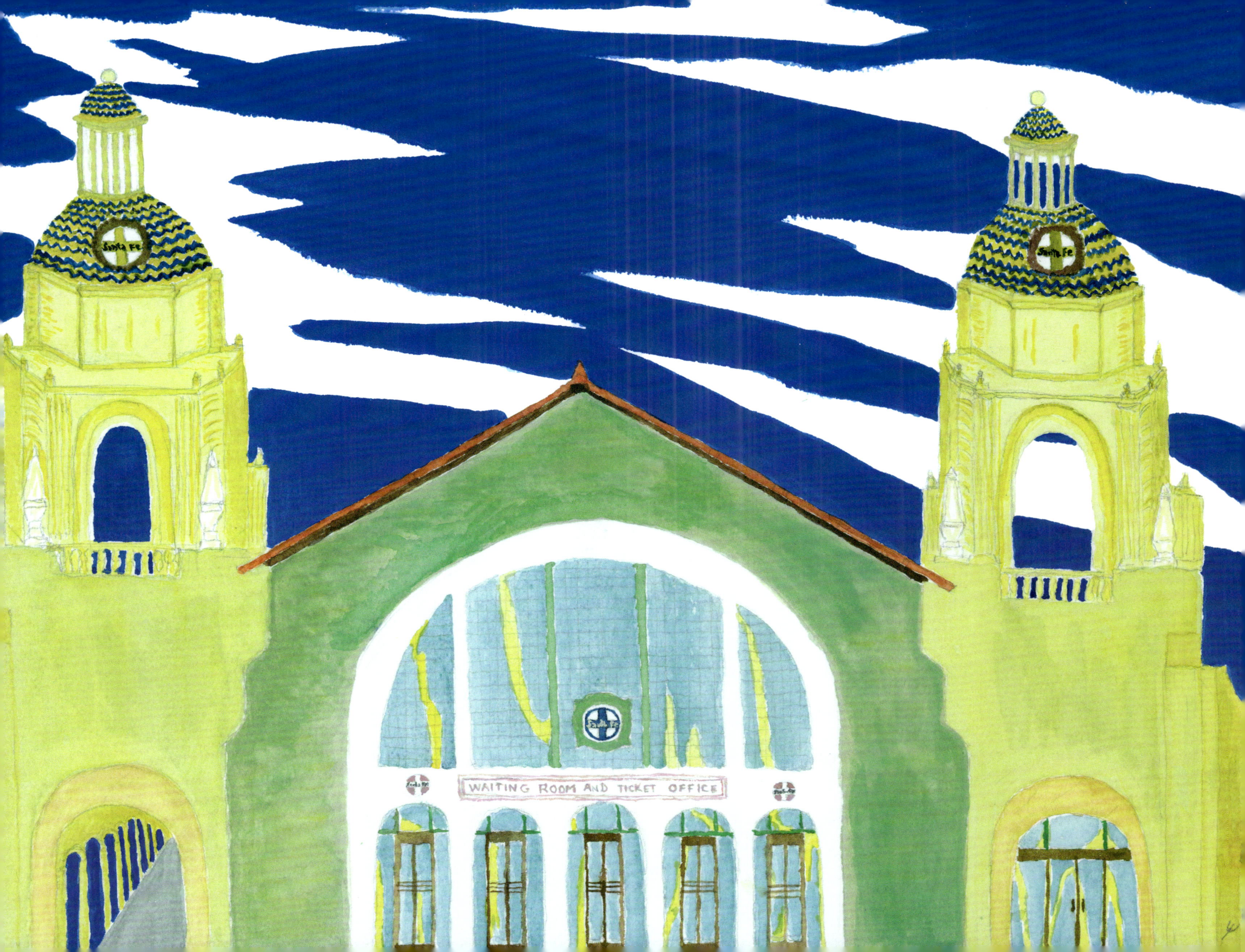
Santa Fe
Santa Fe
WAITING ROOM AND TICKET OFFICE

Great Grandfathers

Tall
palm trees
in the fog,
grizzled old men
who sway
and mutter
to themselves,
stand
along the coast,
while the sun
melts
in mist,
and the palms
enjoy cool breezes
that comb out
their beards.

Dressing Up at Dawn

An old man,
gazing out
at the ocean
early in the morning,
laughs
as he watches
the waves
dance and tumble,
overjoyed
as they leap
under the sunlight,
while the old man
smiles
at the shaving cream
that they have left
adorning their beards.

Stepping Out

Green shores
slope down
to the ocean,
while a palm tree
flirts,
waving its breeze-manicured
fans.

The waves
in bright light
signal
their favor,
their bright-eyed
smile,
for the laughter
of a land
that flaunts
newly-sewn
skirts.

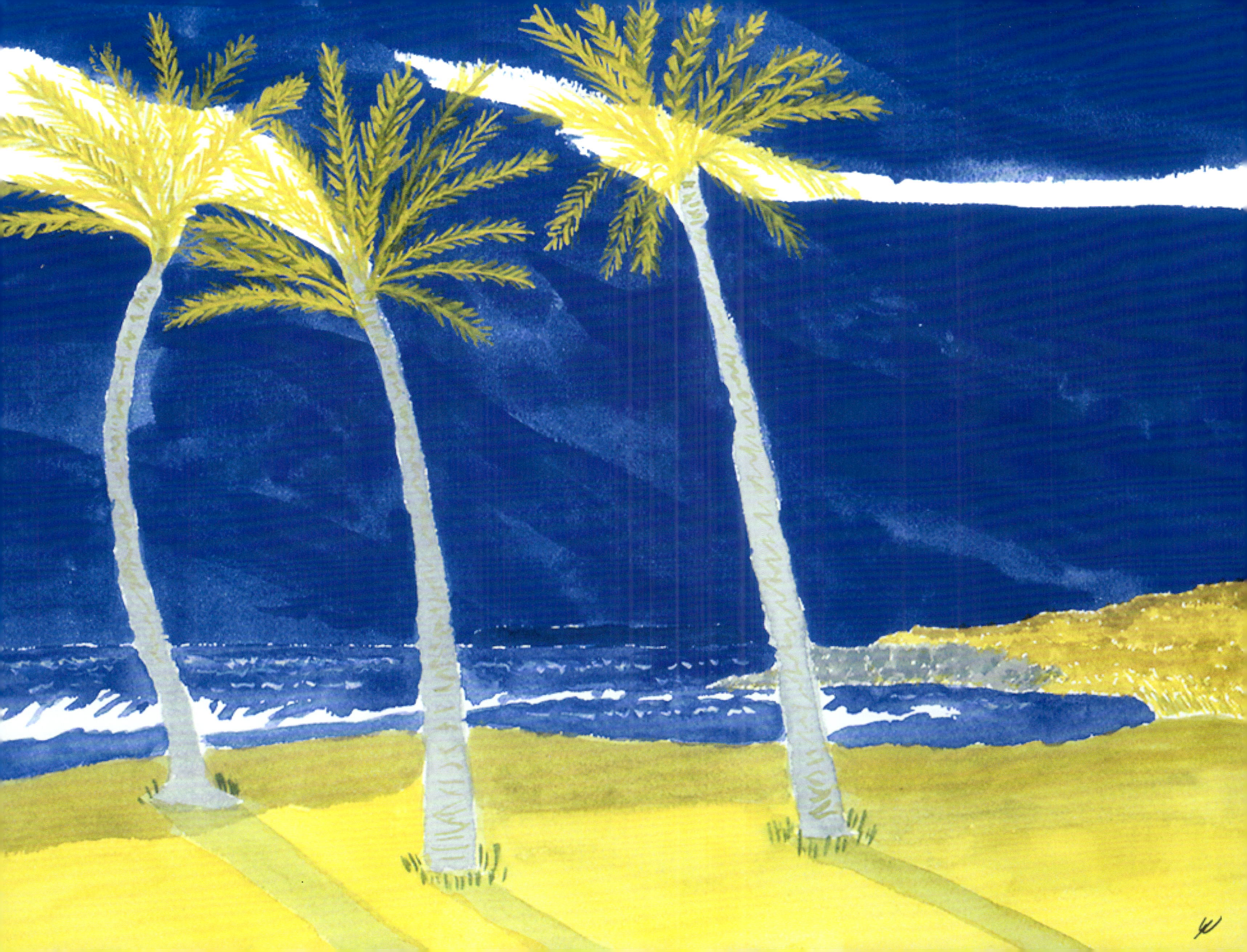

Distractions

An old woman
with wrinkled hands
sits on a park bench,
allowing her fingers
to embrace
one another –
on a green afternoon,
she basks
in the shadows,
savoring
the cool air
and her stare
at the horizon,
until an ancient elm tree
hurls
a grizzled leaf
into her lap,
and she touches
its veined skin,
as soft
as a wedding veil.

Before Easter

A squadron
of snails
crosses
the sidewalk,
inching their way
into a flower bed –
after the rain,
what could be sweeter
than to plunge
into paradise,
with a fresh coat
of sunlight
on your storm-hardened
back?

Serious Enough

The park
of all the days,
quiet
at last
in the late afternoon,
welcomes
the tittering
of an absentminded
fountain,
with its breathless news
of cloistered
laughter.

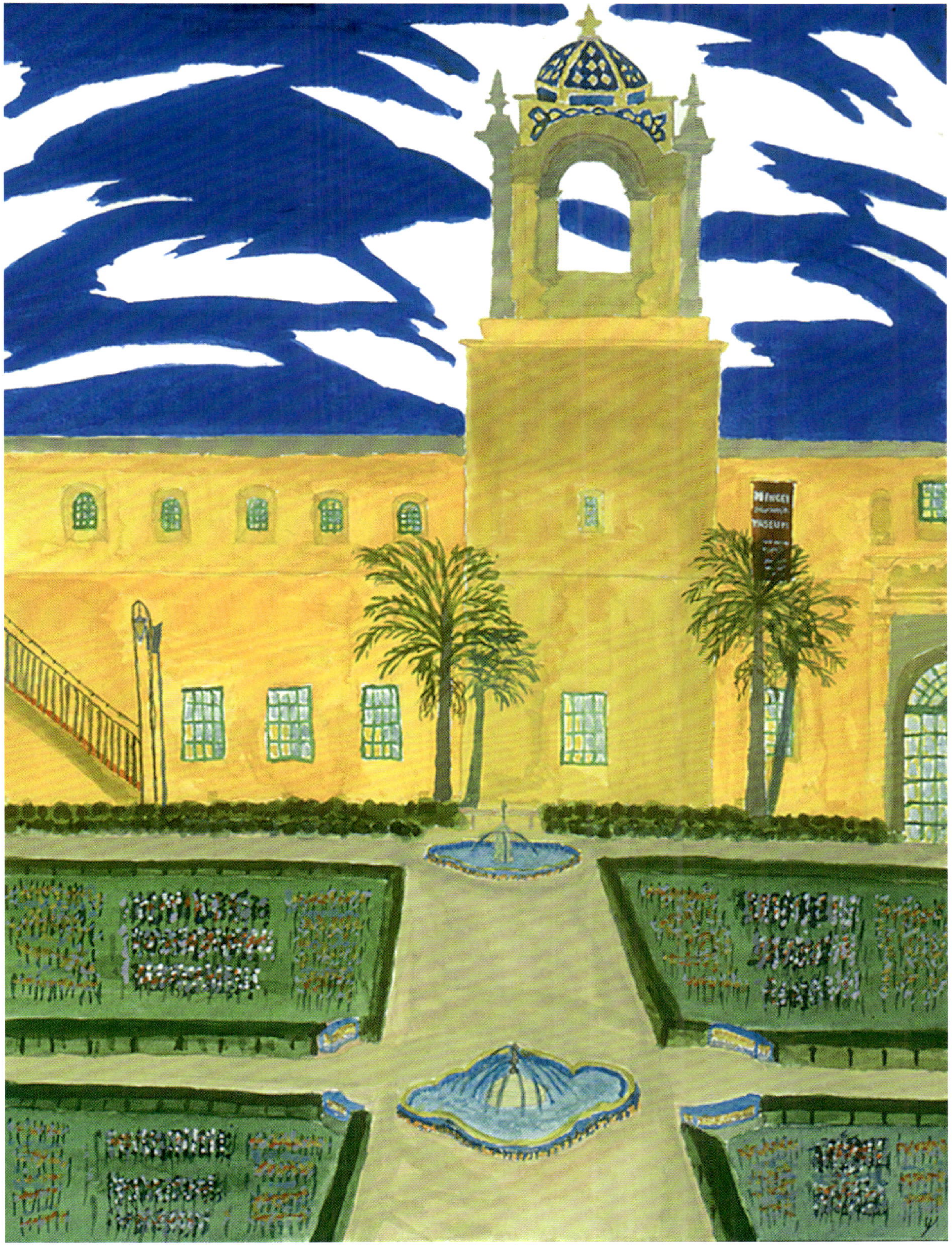

Hand-Me-Down Blessings

Sunlight,
crawling
across the grass,
lends
a wall
a tangerine smile,
and a flower
at its foot
a shadow
to bestow
on the ground,
as an orchid
bouquet
with wings.

A Line of Fire

A tan wall
near the beach
waits
for the sunlight
to pamper it,
and if the fog
prevails
all day,
the rough
stucco wall
will find a way
to beam,
even before
a streetlight
flickers on,
bestowing
its golden-eyed
compliments.

A Kind Wand

On a long
afternoon,
sunlight
plays tag
with a wall,
and, touching
the flat stucco,
turns it
into a field
of goldenrods.

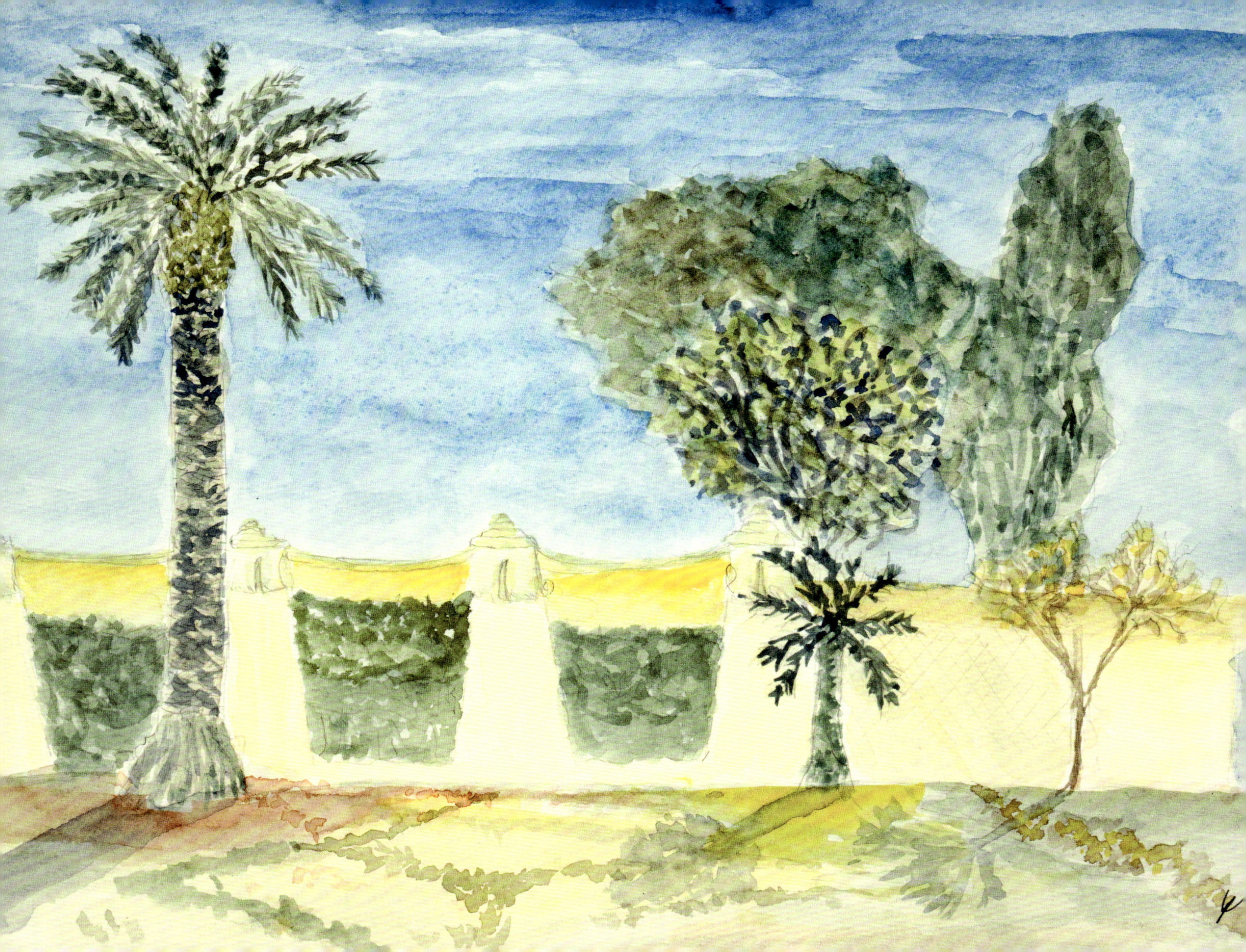

Making the Grade

The ocean
climbs
the stairs
of the shore,
step by step,
wave by wave,
until, reaching
the top,
it tumbles back
into its foam bed
with a roar
of laughter.

Valuables

I carry my dad
in his wallet –
cash, some receipts,
credit cards, IDs –
all neatly stowed
in the brown calfskin
billfold –
compact and in order,
the mementos
welcome
my fingertips,
in the sunlight
that gives them
a chance
to explore
the world
that he escaped,
with a laugh
and never
a glance
backward,
or a tug
at his back pocket.

A Lofty Home

Houses
climb a hill,
snaking their way
toward the summit,
but before they reach it,
a forest
crops up,
crowning the heights
with a green hat
that needs no shelter
from the sky.

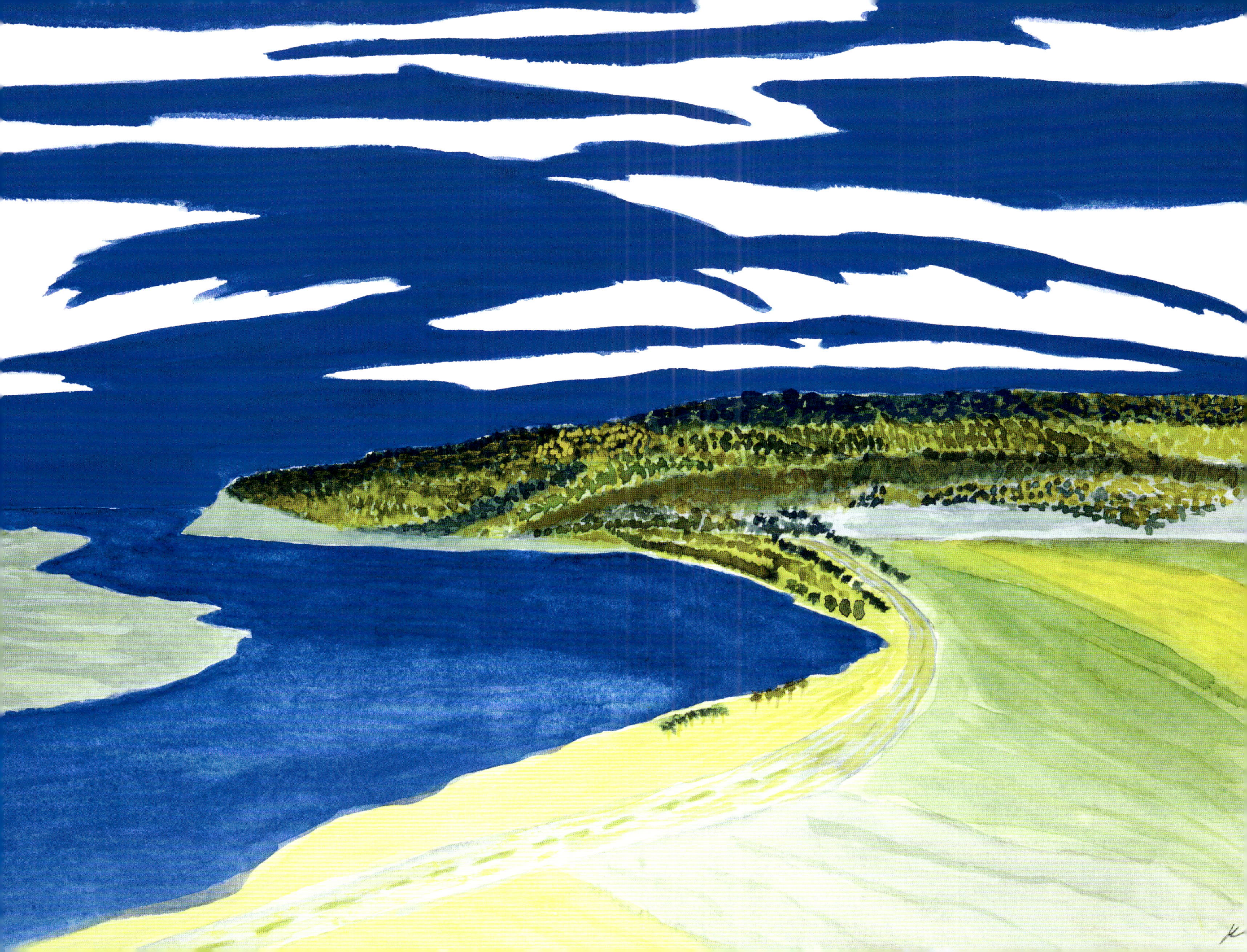

Poetic Trysts

High clouds
meet
and separate,
eternal
drifters
who chat
about love,
then agree
to weep
elsewhere.

Thanksgiving Hope

Thin November light,
miserly
with its smiles,
rests
in the arms
of fiery-eyed trees,
which shake
their heads
before northern winds,
on a day
when shadows
huddle
together,
as the afternoon
fades
to evening,
and the sky
settles down,
to count out
a fortune
in stars.

The Big Show

The twilight sky
fades
into lilac,
then orchid,
then turquoise,
then aquamarine,
and when the land
has slipped
under its gray
and green comforter,
the sky
casts
a host of glances
through moth holes
in a tattered tent
of indigo
silk.

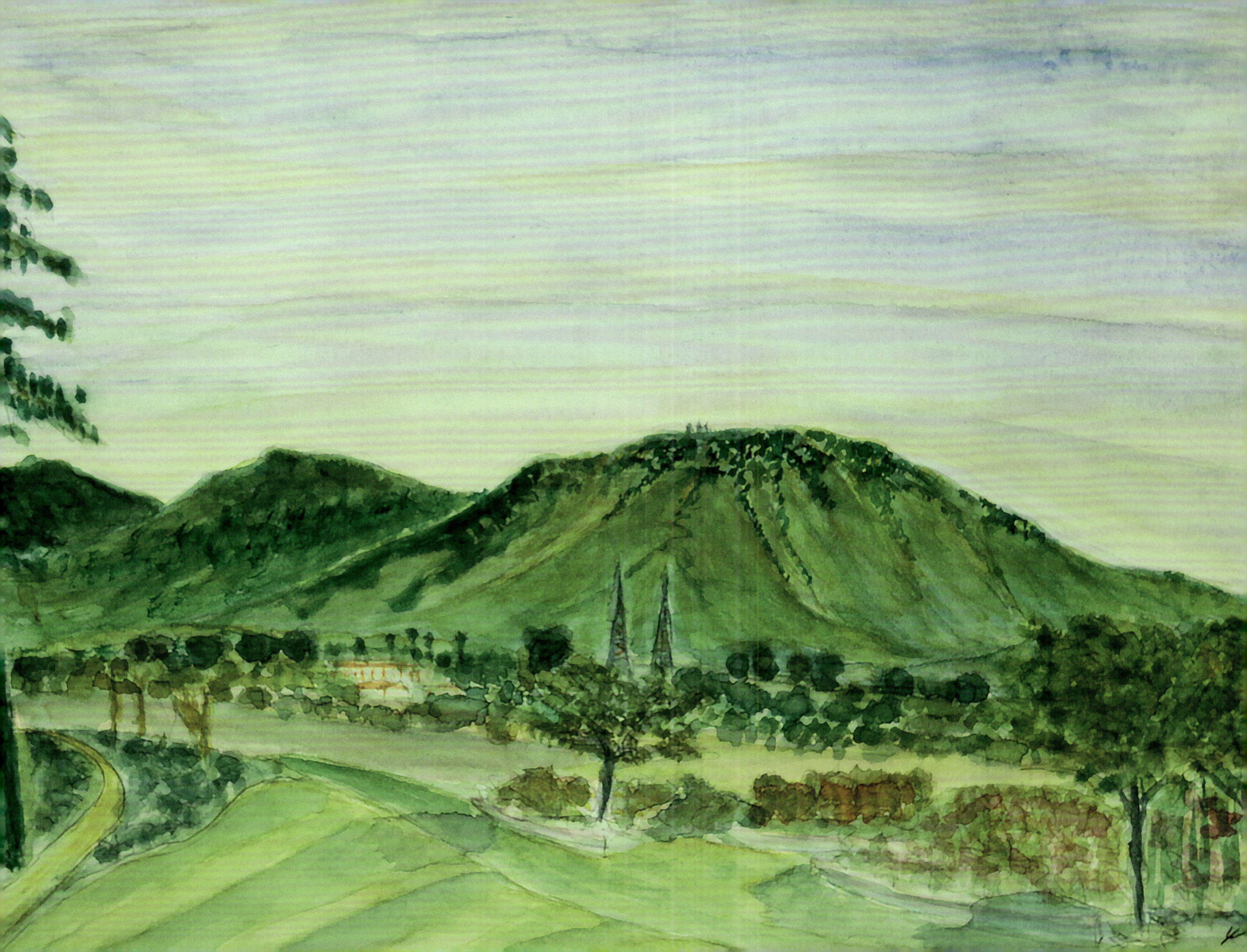

Lending a Hand

Leaves
all about you,
fallen
on the pavement,
offer
their upturned smiles,
like red
and yellow
mittens.

Shades of Blue

A bluebird,
pecking at the grass,
dances,
to give thanks
for a lawn sprinkler
that hisses,
as it spits out
its opinion
of a sky
with no clouds.

The Course of Things

Honeysuckle,
biding its time
under a summer
fog,
spreads
its perfume
in early morning,
then waits
for passersby
to slacken
their pace,
sighing
as they mull over
bygone
loves.

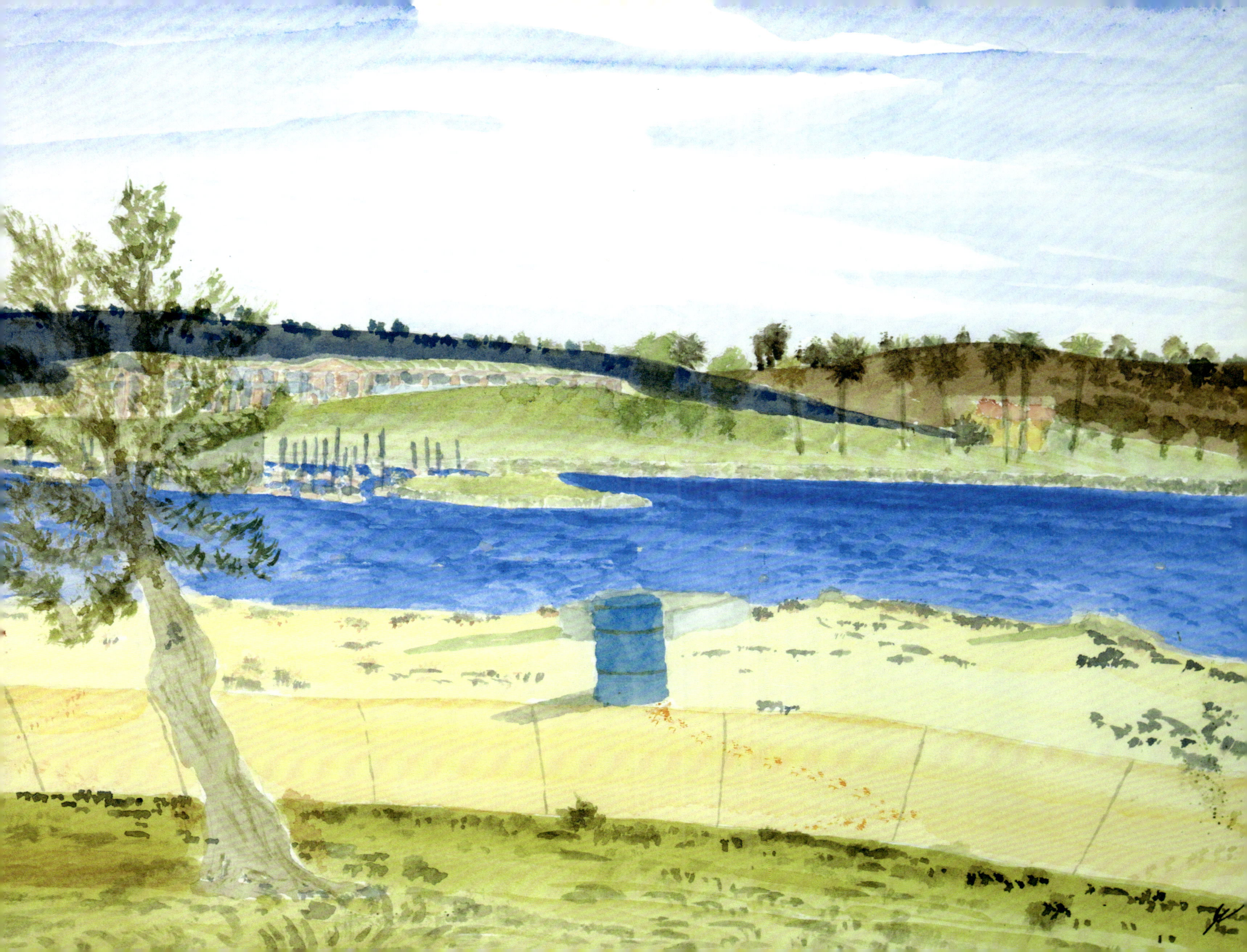

Unexpected Blessings

A distant
pool
of light
floats
upon the ocean.

I outstretch
my hand
to touch it,
then pull it back
with a cool
lake
of sky
in my palm.

A Change of Pace

A golden sunset
over the coast
lends the land
a brilliant lining
of embroidery –
the hills
take off
their blue and green
dressing coats,
and settle
for dark purple
pajamas.

A Stouthearted Suitor

The long dusk,
golden
and generous,
holds its own
for hour after hour,
not giving in
to the high canopy
of stars,
for it will not yield
to any
far-flung light,
for here,
at its fingertips,
is a bouquet
of sunflowers.

Sunset, Mission Bay

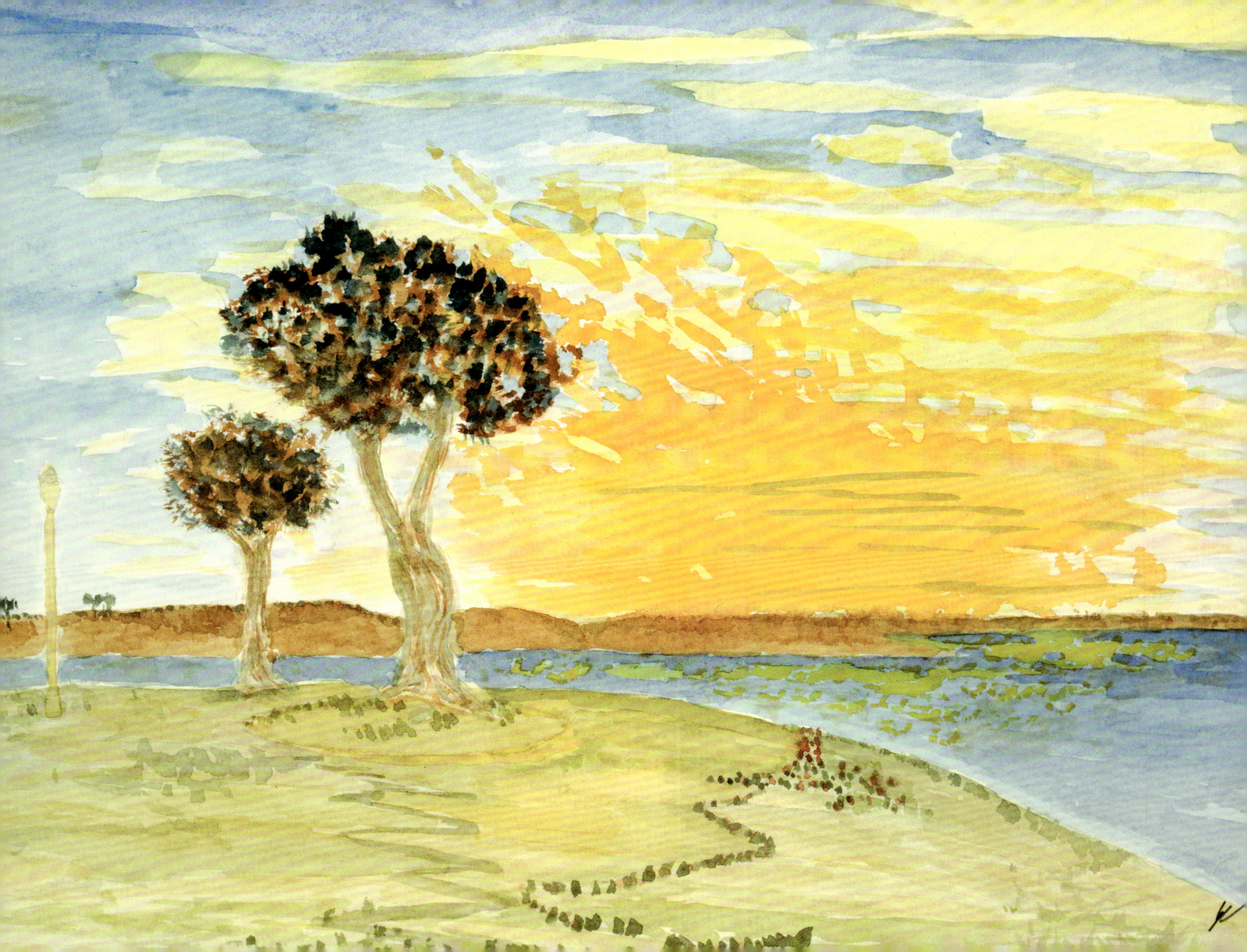

Circus Stars

A quiet day
beside the bay
softens
the sky
into a high tent
with blue and white
stripes,
while sailboats
glide
among soft breezes,
and the light,
setting sail
for western islands,
balances
on its trapeze,
before performing
a triple
somersault,
into the laps
of applauding
waves.

Any Port in a Calm

A blue harbor,
opening
its arms
to embrace
the ocean,
smiles
at seafaring ships
that glide toward the shore,
seeking
a fair-weather
lover.

A Bright Blue Road

And still
the calm-eyed
ocean
welcomes
would-be voyagers
in May,
for they,
setting forth
with their longing gazes,
leave caution
to other months,
when the ocean
is a blur
of landward
gray
glances.

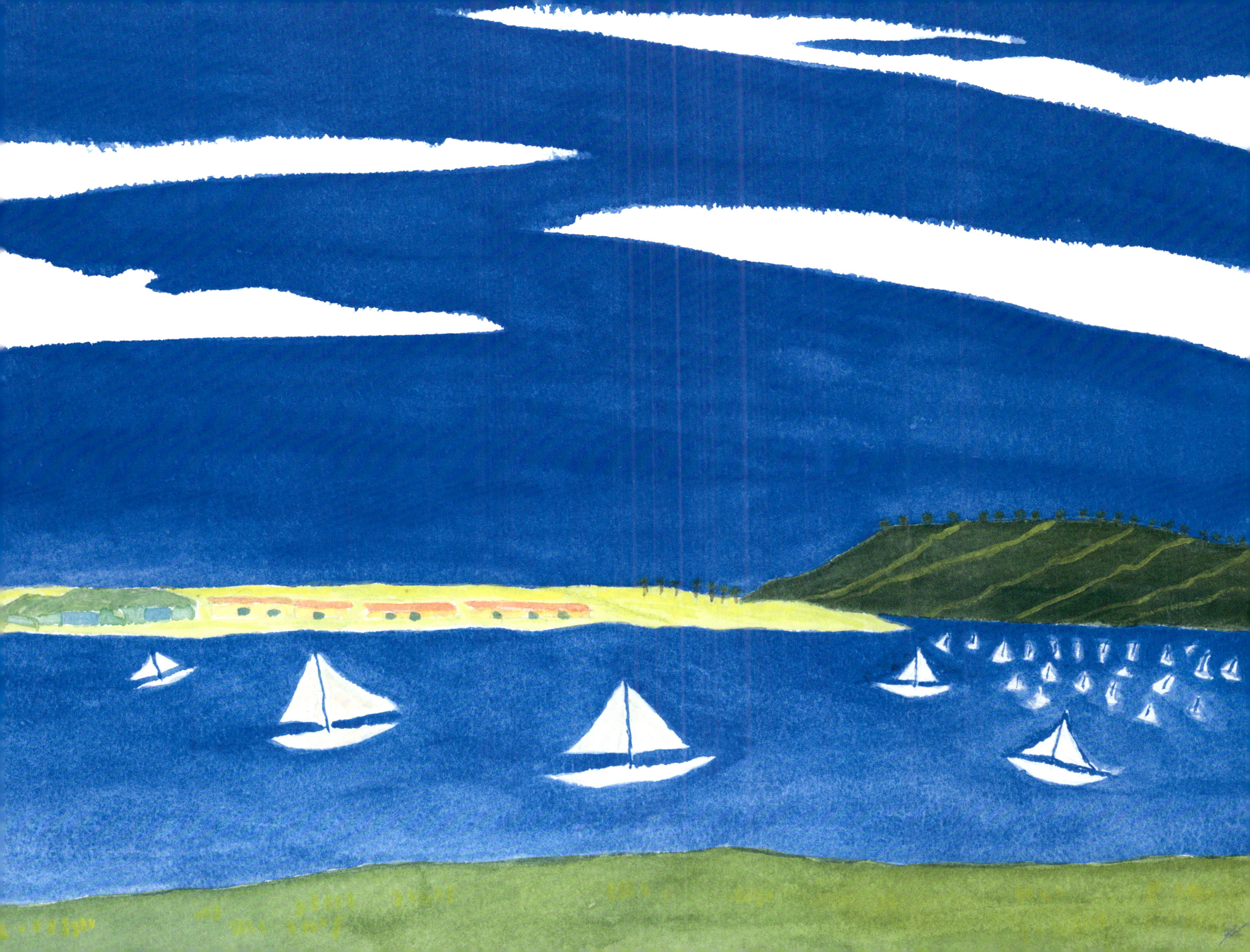

A Vast Dictionary

A young man
hoists
his toddler daughter
in his arms,
to point out
birds and flowers
and somersaulting
leaves –
naming them all,
one by one,
he watches her
smile,
as she outstretches her hands –
sunlight tumbles
onto her fingertips,
which touch the soft air,
while her father
embraces the silence.

An Autumn Stroll

An old man,
his face framed
by gray hair,
trundles
though the park,
smiling
at the golden leaves –
patiently they pirouette
from branches
to the yellowing grass,
while he,
taking the hand
of the wandering sunlight,
makes his way
through the lazy park,
which welcomes his slow footsteps,
as he gives up
the comfort
of benches,
for the company
of his own wandering shadow,
never at home
with any path
that does not meander,
to catch sight
of a high-limbed
evergreen.

Answering Heaven

A confusion
of toddlers,
holding
hands,
drifts
down a sunlit path,
where the children
sing out
their chorus
of words,
in praise
of the sky,
the birds,
the bay,
the worms,
the leaves,
the stones,
the clouds,
and one another's
laughter.

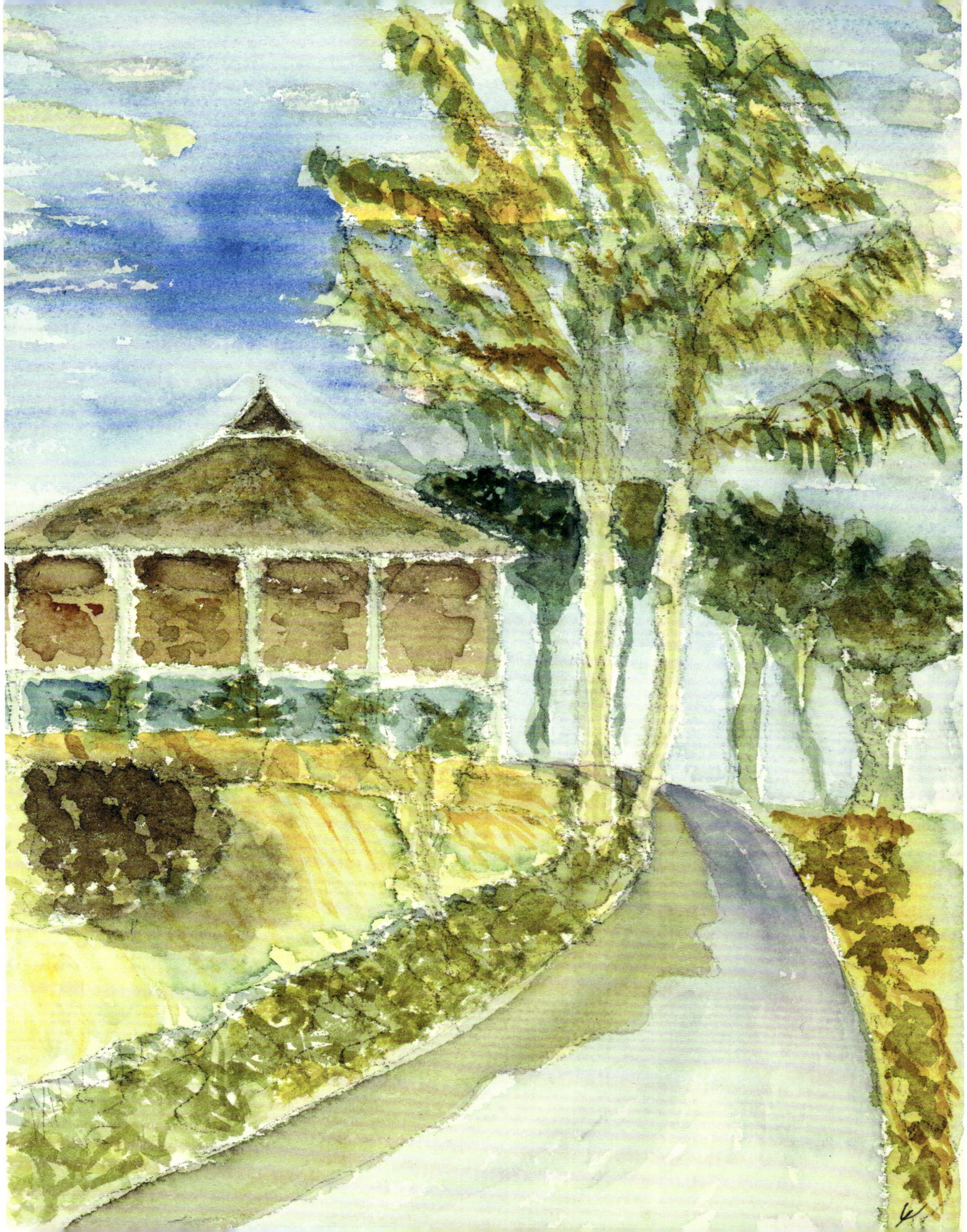

Fame

Leaves
leave their fingerprints
all over the sidewalk –
yellow
and black
and brown
and red –
after the storm,
they mark the pavement
with their signatures,
while they rest
in the fragrant grass,
where breezes
have opened
a new book
for them.

Mixed Blessings

A bee
that has died
in the back
of my car,
on a scorching day
in summer,
perches
near the window,
and now,
under gray
autumn skies,
shines
as brilliantly
as the sun,
his orbit
generous
to me,
his weaponry
forever
disarmed,
and with it
his festive
drumroll.

Roller Coaster

A middle-aged woman
skateboards
down the street,
with her red hair
creeping out
from beneath her helmet –
rounding a corner,
she laughs
at a patch of sunlight
that has camped out
on the sidewalk,
just a few feet
from where the broad street
tumbles
down the hill,
with its houses' rooftops
lifting high
their manicured
red fingernails.

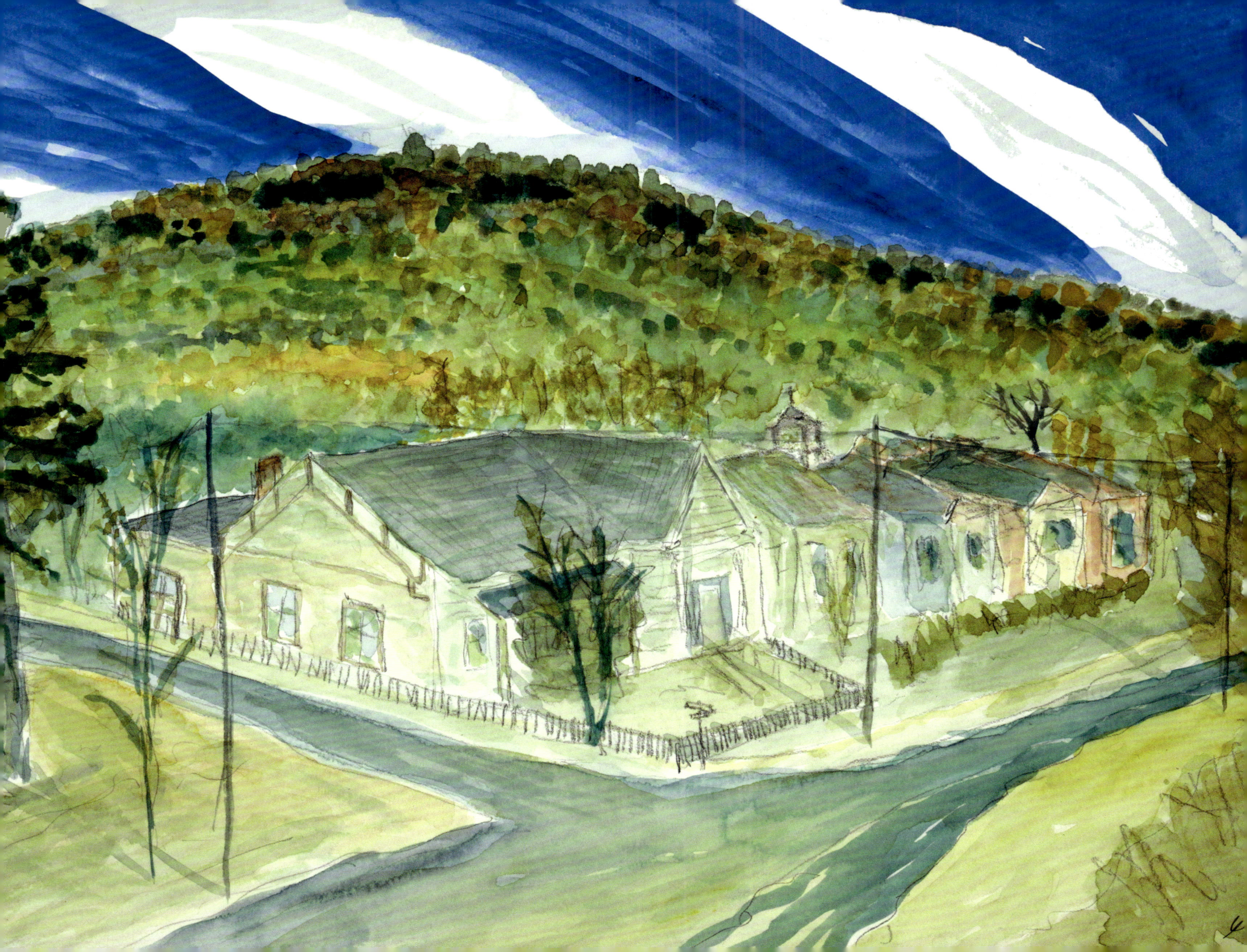

High Rollers

A mountain valley,
basking
in sunlight,
opens its arms
to the shadows
of clouds,
which glide
across the tawny land
with gray fingertips
that tickle
the treetops.

Formal Attire

Mountains
unfurl
their skirts
of white fog,
with satin ribbons
and taffeta hems –
rough-skinned
old ladies,
with no pretense
of beauty,
they dress
for the occasion,
for the day's
daily waltz,
to be asked
for a dance
by an old beau,
a sky
with a blue silk
tuxedo.

A Soft Wardrobe

Blue mountains
above the desert
change clothes
minute by minute,
tossing
aside
richly-woven
shadows,
to don
blue jeans
bleached
by a sun
clad only
in tattered
clouds.

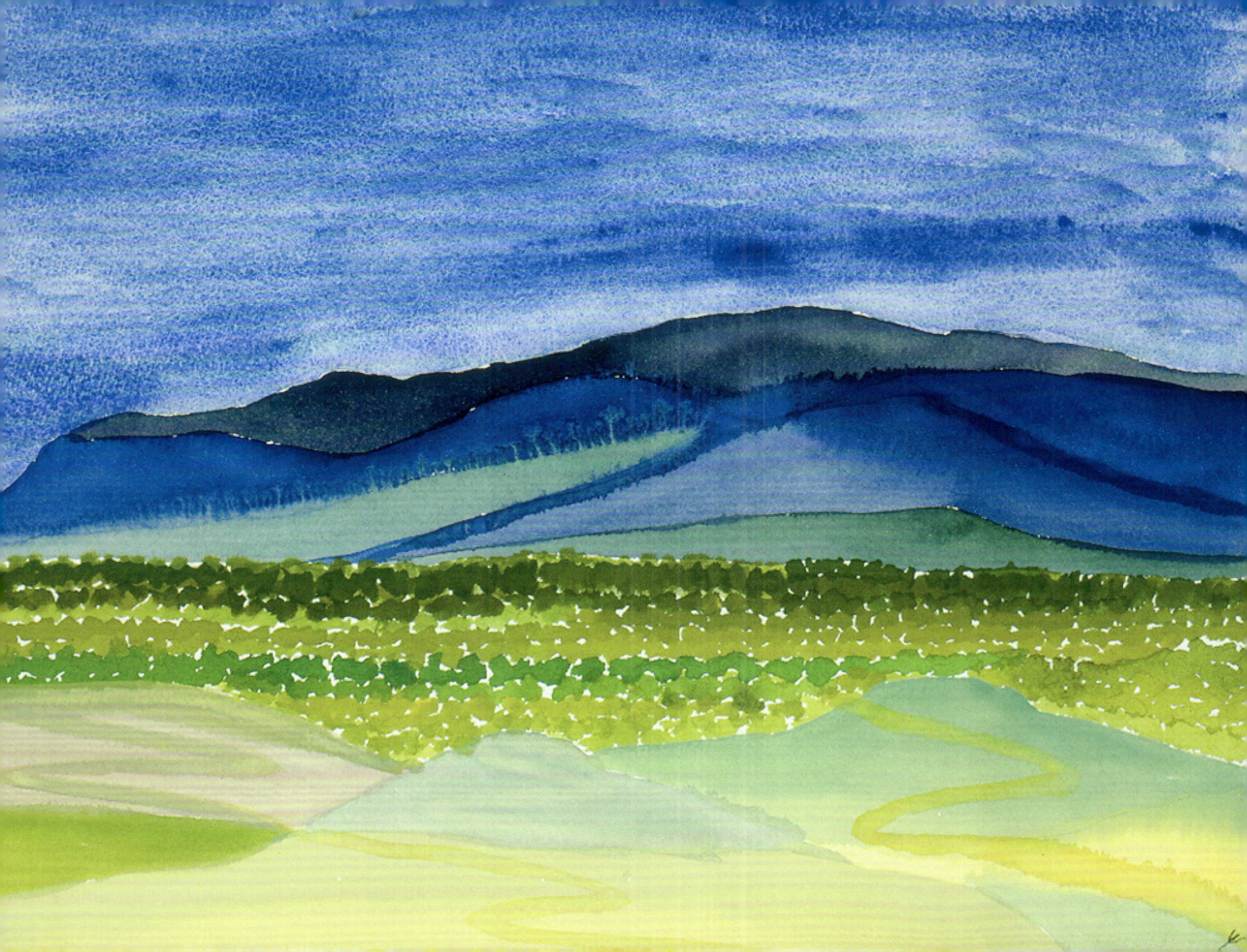

A Whirlwind Romance

A quiet
courtyard
in winter
welcomes
the lazy
sunlight,
and the shadows
that dance
with one another,
beside a fountain
that titters
about breezes
adorned
with scarlet
leaves.

September Song

In the park
of all the days,
two lovers
hug
forever –
standing in the sunlight,
they caress
each other's backs,
sharing the warmth
of their wordless bodies,
as the fountain
jabbers,
and dogs yelp
at one another,
and a friendly swing
squeaks,
and the traffic
grumbles –
in the midst
of all the busy world,
they hold one another,
supporting
their silence,
and do not care
where the sidewalk leads,
or how many strangers
fail to meet,
on a sunlit day
in the fall.

Autumn Blessings

Sitting
in the sunshine
under a sky
boasting
lazy clouds,
you listen
to a fountain
sputter
its complaints,
as you lean back
and watch sparrows
peck
at the thinning grass,
where a sprinkling
of seeds
and blossoms
entrust their fates
to the wind.

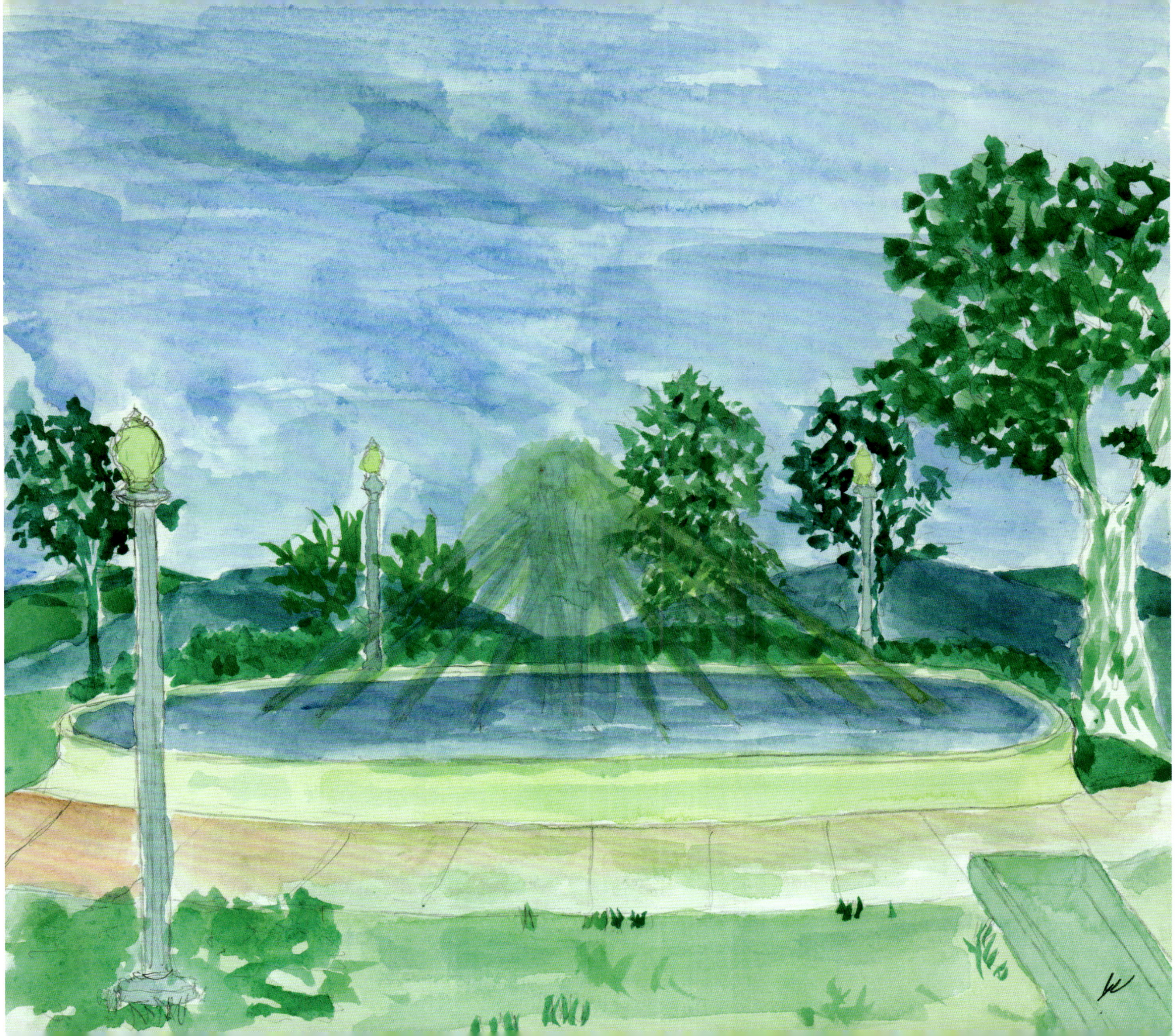

Partners

Two roses,
one high,
one low
on a rosebush,
mingle
their bittersweet perfume,
until no one
notices
which blossom
bleeds red,
and which one
bandages
the wound
with white gauze.

An Epic Journey

A caterpillar,
crossing the driveway,
takes twelve steps
at a time,
then inches along,
arching his back,
as he makes his way
across the rough concrete,
to a promised land
of soft-spoken
grass.

Inside Out

A college hall,
all bravado
and baroque
braggadocio,
beams
in the autumn
sunlight,
so kind
to wrinkles
and crevices,
behind which
wisdom
may flourish,
with only a glance
out a wide-eyed
window.

Camino Hall, U.S.D.

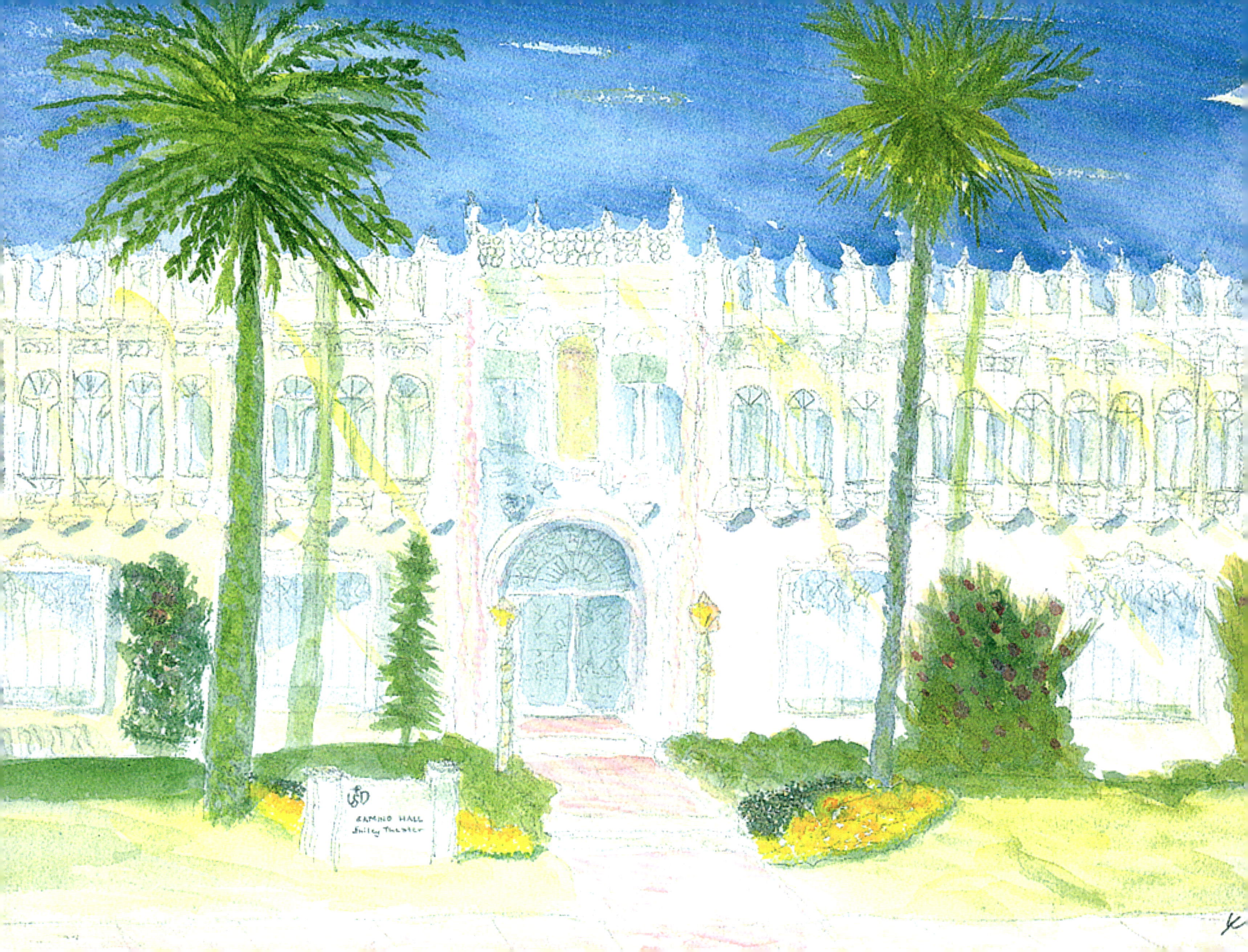
CAMINO HALL
Shiley Theater

Purple Pleasures

Wisteria
blossom
in a tardy spring,
drooping
their lavender blossoms
from trellises –
patient dreamers
in the arms
of breezes,
they wait
for the sunlight
to grow drowsy,
and rest
on the shoulders
of early bloomers.

Competition

A lonely bee
keeps me company,
as I paint
every day
in the park –
hovering
about my hands,
he wishes
that my brushstrokes
would be tinged
with sweet colors,
and when I
close up shop,
he seeks out
a blossom
that has dyed itself
scarlet,
and doused itself
in perfume,
to rub in
my artistic
shortcomings.

Company

Bougainvillea
in blossom,
hanging down
from a gray
park shelter,
festoon
faded
wooden posts
with a sky
that wears
lavender
eyeshade.

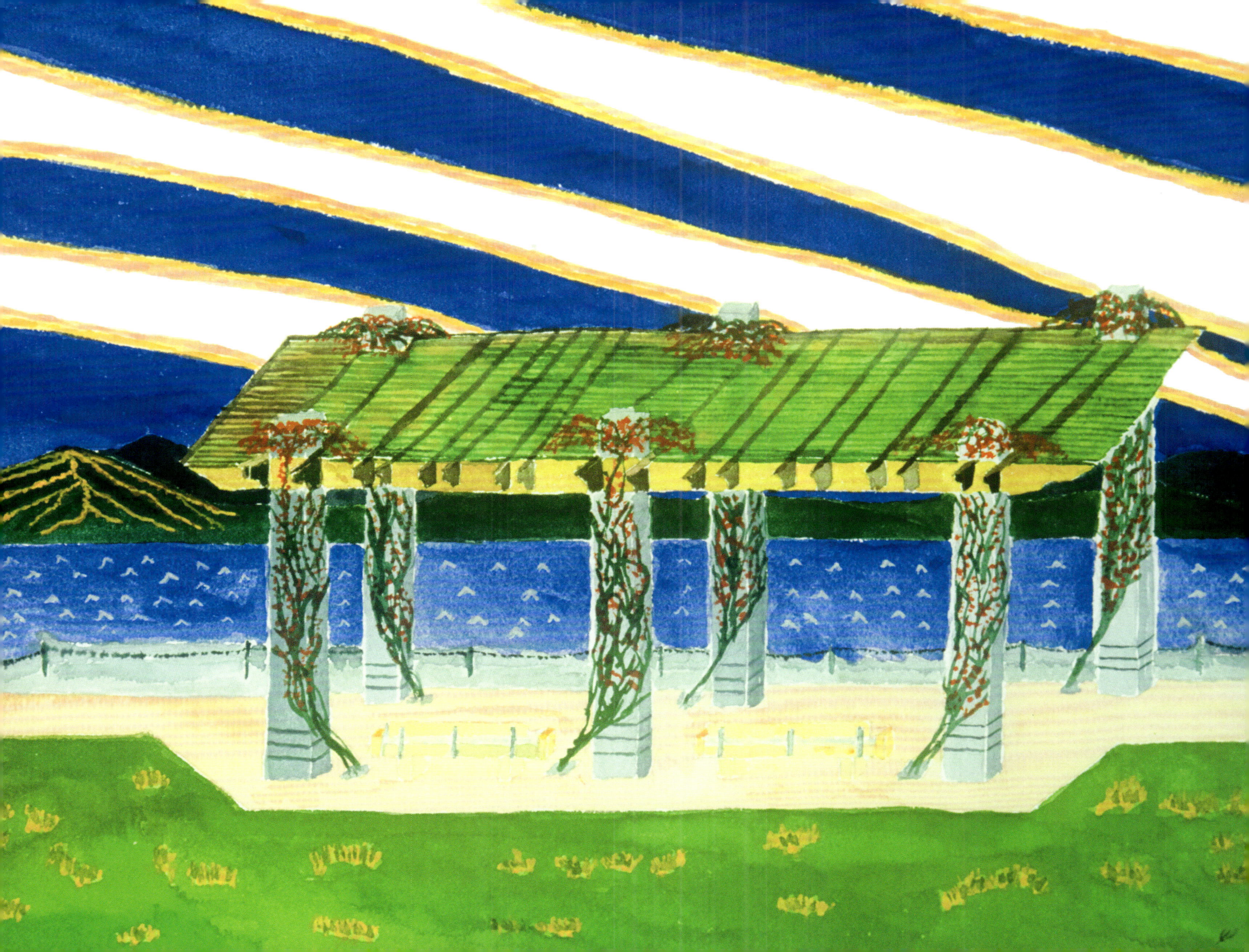

Faithful Gardeners

Dewdrops
glisten
at dawn
on the faces
of fallen
leaves –
clear-eyed
sentinels,
they watch
the sky
blossom,
into a bouquet
of blue
and rose
hydrangea.

Un-walling a Garden

Stopping
to smell
a blossom
that the lady
who tended roses
once nurtured,
you smile
at its storm-wrinkled
petals,
and touch the soft skin
that breezes
enfold –
its scent
barely lingers,
as it bobs
in the sunlight,
while the woman
who cherished it
now tends
only her home,
with no need
to remind gardeners
how few days
calm hands
have.

A Retiring Lady

A rosebush
flourishes
beside the wall
of a house –
even in shyness,
it lifts high
its yellow blossoms,
flirtatious
with morning sunlight,
and with afternoon shadows
that dote
on perfume.

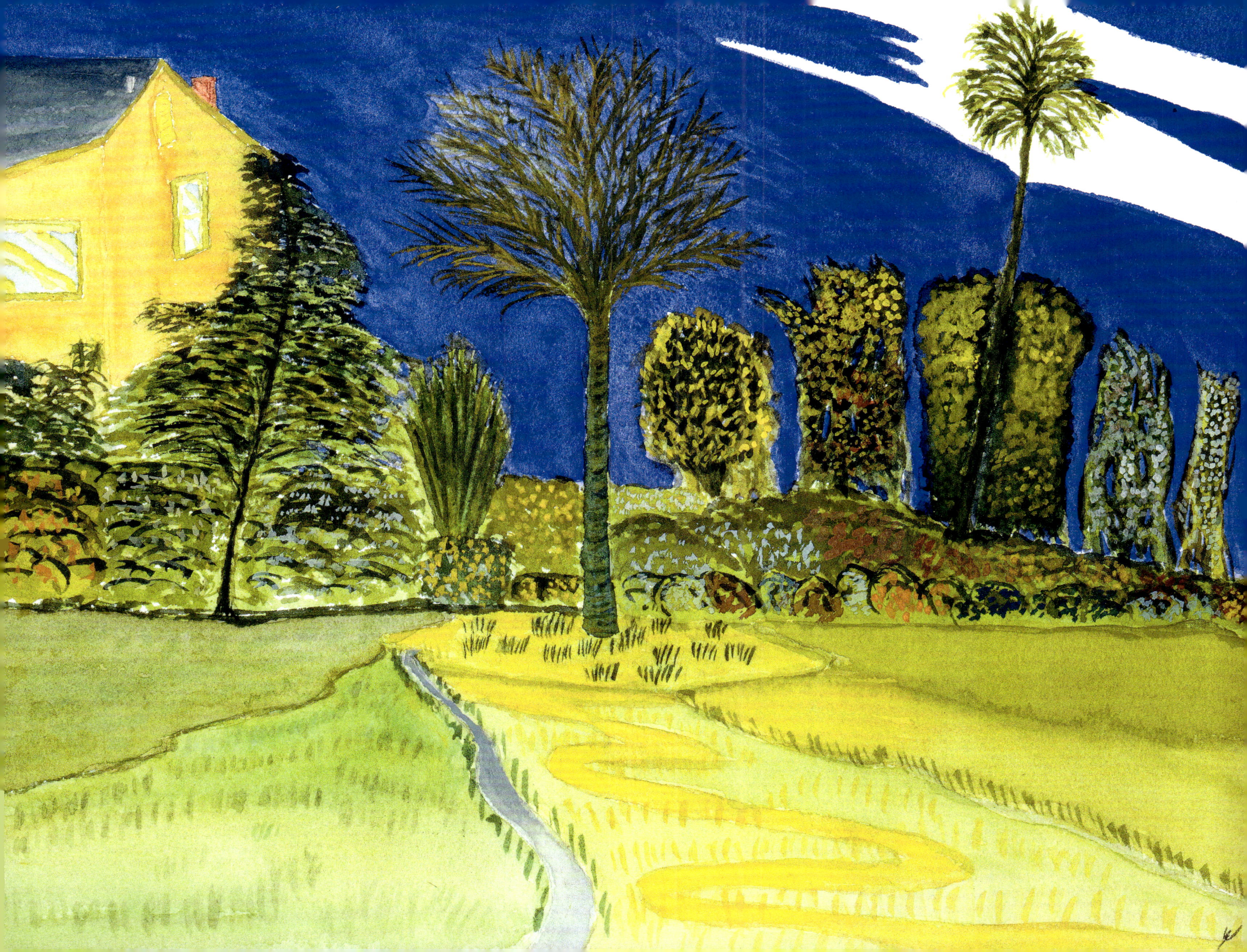

Coastal Daydreams

A quiet day
beside the bay
welcomes
the green hills,
the calm ocean,
the overarching
light,
while boats lollygag
among calm waves,
and breezes
tug at flags,
and heights
that have softened
their hearts
to tawny meadows
gaze out
at the blue bay,
which has settled
into a quiet corner,
where it reflects
the gaze
of a gentle-eyed
sky.

Fresh Air

Sailboats'
riggings
twitter to each other
in a winter
rainstorm,
telegraphing
one another
their news
of distant ports,
until the clouds
part,
and you glimpse
a downpour
of stars,
and the ropes
and halyards
and pulleys
and blocks
whisper
to masts
of their loneliness
for gasping sails.

Polite Awakenings

Sailboats
glide across the bay,
as beach homes
awaken
to the sputtering
of the tide –
on a hill
in the distance,
a flag
snaps to attention,
while the sky
rolls over
to doze,
and the ocean
nudges the shore
with an elbow
of light.

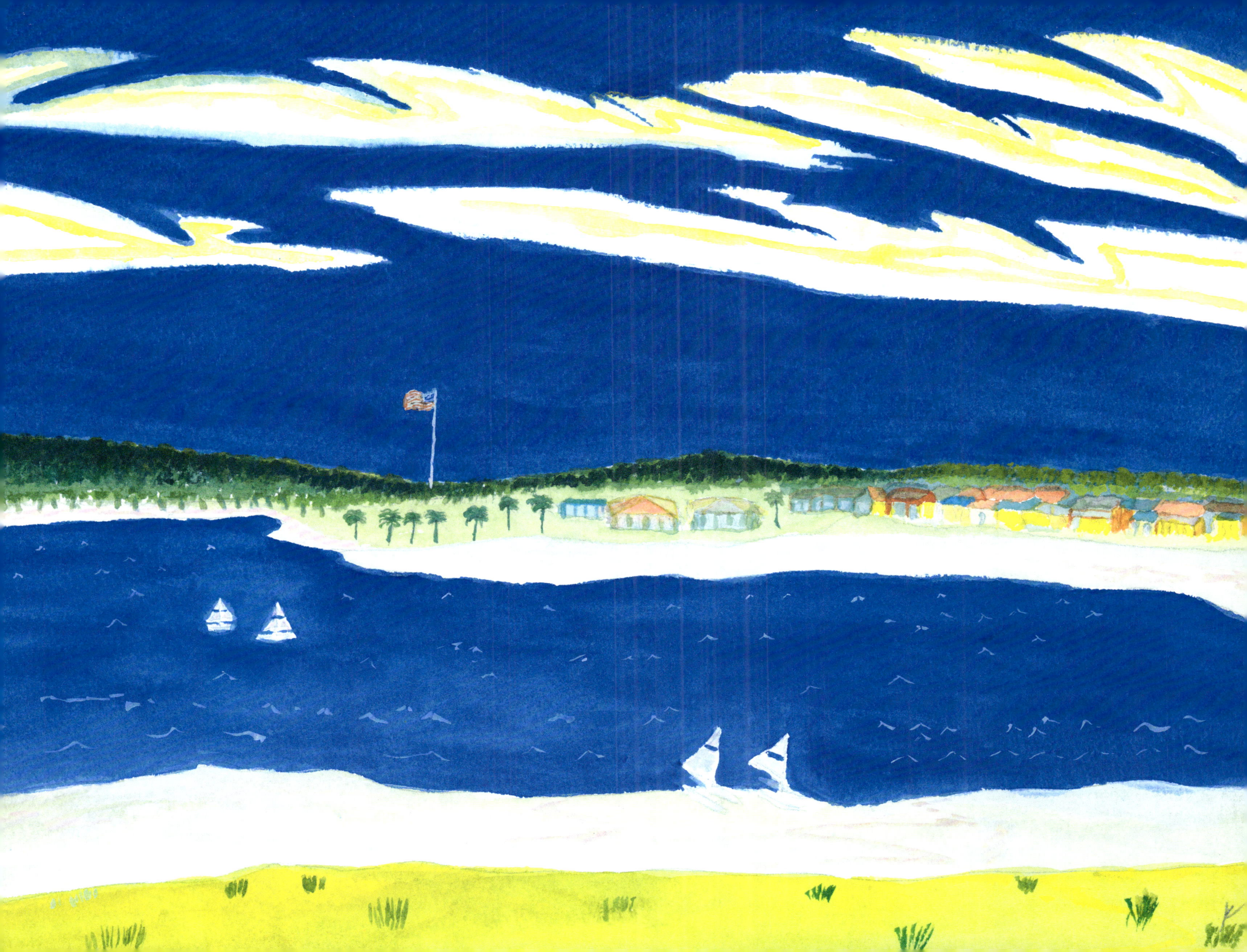

Touchdown

The teenaged boy
with a heart
that he has outgrown,
the boy
who used
to play varsity
football,
and now cannot,
smiles
in the gym
as he turns
to his exercise,
and, recalling
a rain-soaked game,
laughs
at the thought
of his slide
through the mud,
past a washed-away
goal line,
into the end zone's
lake.

Fire in the Gut

A young rebel
with long legs
and a blue
baseball cap
smirks
as he sits in the dentist's
waiting room,
sprawling
in a chair,
while he boasts
to a stranger
that he was kicked out
of summer high school,
but is returning
in the fall;
stretching out
and smiling,
with every fiber
in his body
aflame,
he dares
the world
to tell him
not to raise hell,
or the dentist
to gloat
over a cavity
or two.

Growing Up

Blue skies
dotted
with pale clouds
smile
at sunlight
that comes calling
on a morning
in spring,
when the ocean
outstretches
its blue and white tablecloth,
and islands
doze off
under canopies
of palm trees –
freighters
trundle
across the horizon,
and seagulls
venture
far from the land –
thunderheads
raise their sails,
and low clouds
plant islands
with their patient shadows.

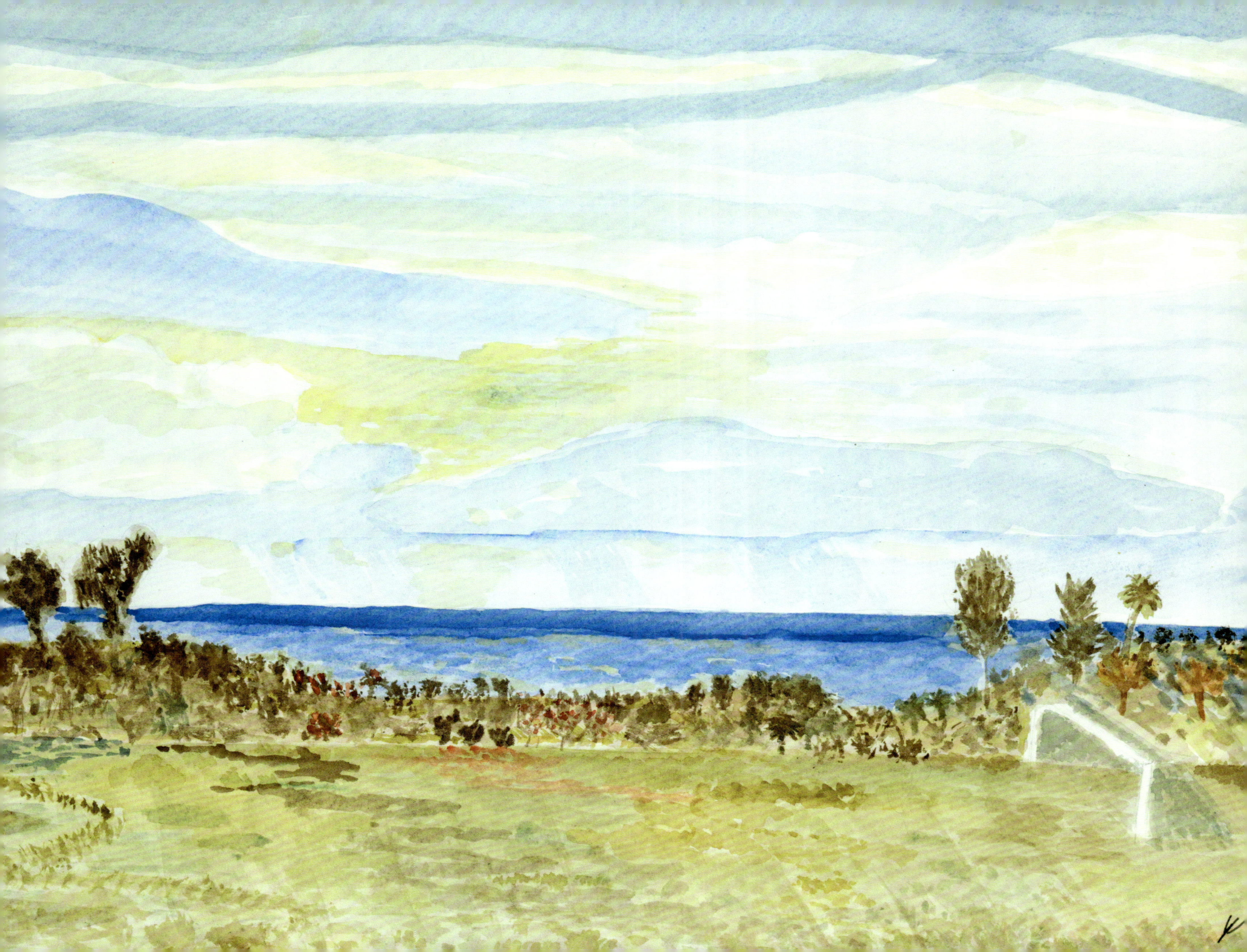

Carrying a Torch

The sun,
an orange smudge
on the cheek
of the horizon,
makes the sky
and the ocean
ardent lovers,
finding
one another
face to face,
as they share
a golden
blush.

Billy

Remembering
a friend,
dead
these twelve years,
you laugh
the laughter
of angels,
and smile
at the thought
of his soft-shoe dance
that lasted
a lifetime.

Late Light

A long
afterglow,
settling
upon the horizon,
calms
ocean waves
with a veil
of spun gold,
a warmhearted
gauze
through which stars
slip,
to keep
their nightly
trysts.

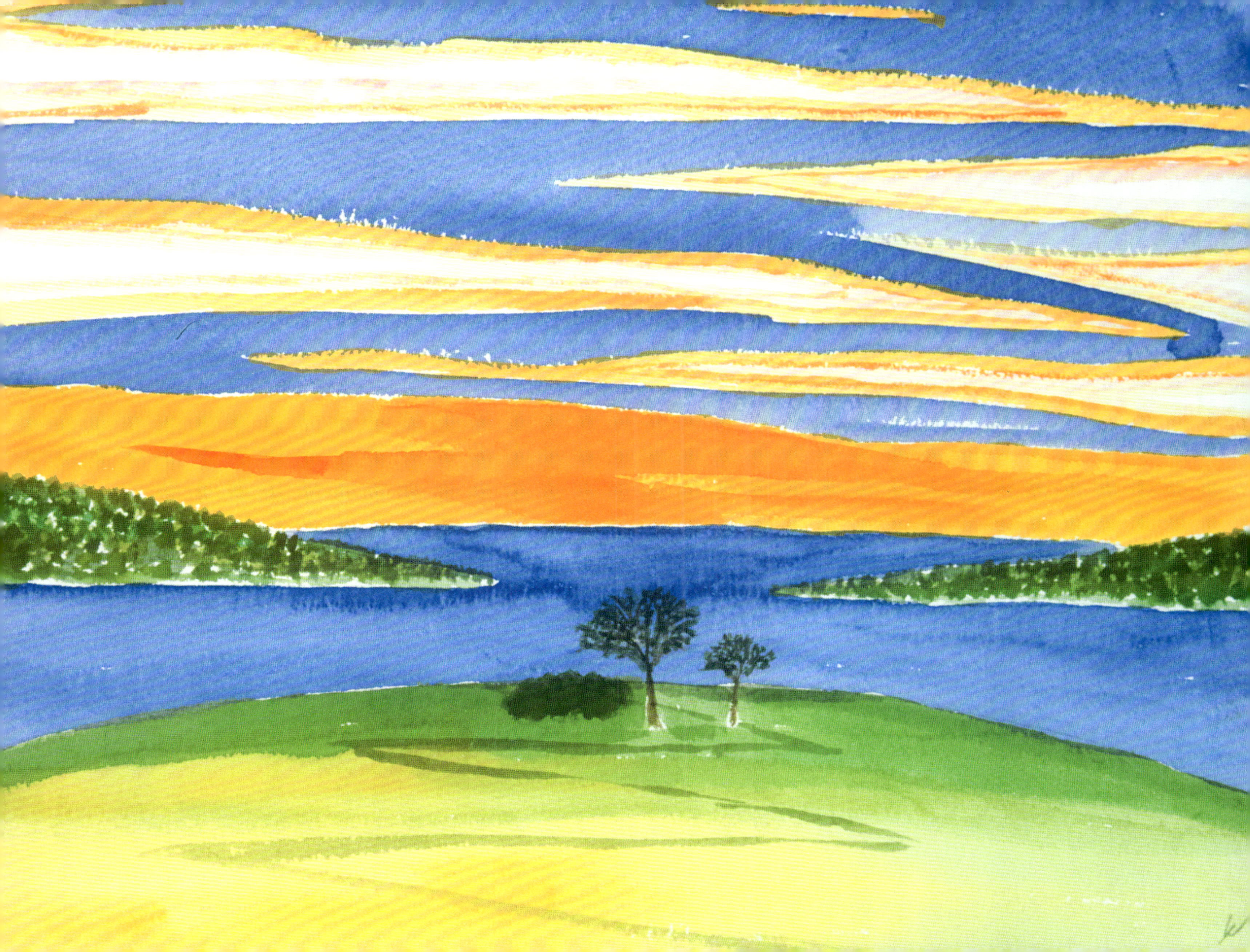

High Marks

A light-faced
fountain
before a dark wall
spits out
its laughter,
its glee
and its giggling,
while beneath it
a blue pool,
as cool-eyed
as the sky,
reflects
the three smiles
of children
who delight
in making
their stony gazes
ripple.

An Unexpected Friend

I thought
that I heard something
drop –
so quietly
that I could not say
what,
and saw no debris
from my inside-out
pocket;
later
I caught sight
of a bright-faced
dime,
lavishing
its smile
on my
down-and-out
eyes.

An Outspoken Friend

The fountain
is my daily
companion,
tittering
and giggling
and choking
back tears,
and gurgling
and hissing
and gushing
about floods,
and grumbling
and guffawing
and sputtering
about sunlight,
and gasping
and whispering
and wishing
out loud,
and always
taking time
to listen
to my laughter,
or, singing out a question,
composing a song
out of my solitary
sighs.

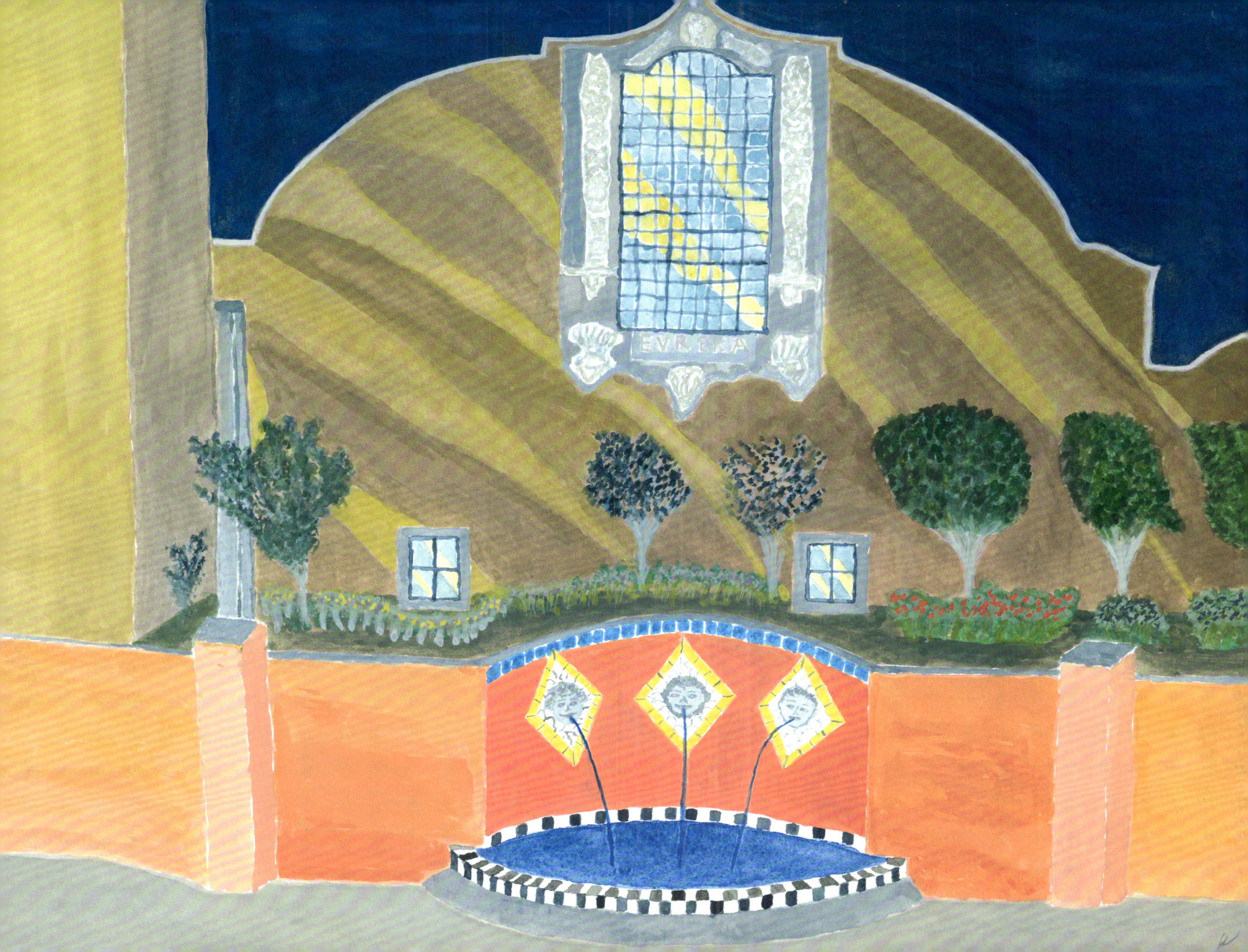
EVREKA

Swimming Home

The ocean
stretches out,
mile after mile,
seeking the land,
and the last
of the clouds –
on a calm day
it finds its way
to a shore
with soft breezes,
and a beach
that the sun
has baptized
with a wayfaring
smile.

Spring Tidings

March rain,
calm
and persistent,
taps
on the roof
all night long –
and in the morning,
when you open
your door,
a clear-eyed
puddle
smiles
at a wayward
cloud.

The Light Fantastic

Beyond the breakers
and the golden cliffs,
and a road
that wriggles
home,
the ocean
follows
its own footsteps,
to a dance floor
where waves sweep
the sky
off its feet.

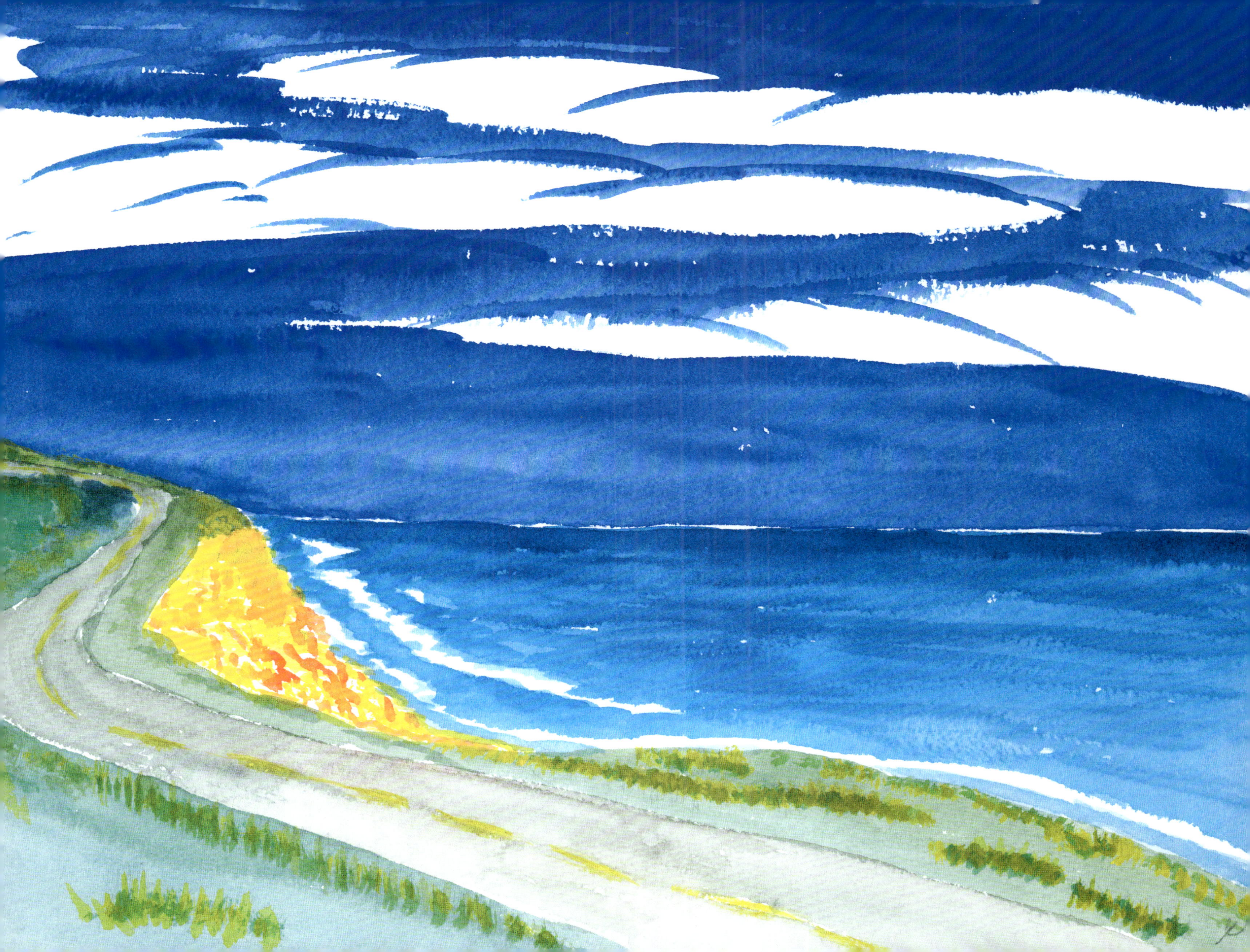

A Letter from Beethoven

At dawn,
you awaken
to a light
as light
as the shadow
of a blue
feather.

Rock 'n' Roll

The gray ocean
tosses and turns
all night long,
unable to sleep
when the moon
comes courting:
high tide
arrives,
blaring,
just after midnight,
and for the rest of the night,
silver light
and waves
strap on
their dancing shoes.

An Act of Will

An old
sailing ship,
moored
in a quiet
harbor,
waits
for its chance
to skip
across the horizon,
then glances
from its dock
at a mirror
of purple water,
in which it puffs out
the cheeks of its sails
and sets a course
for an ocean
where whales
still
dance with waves.

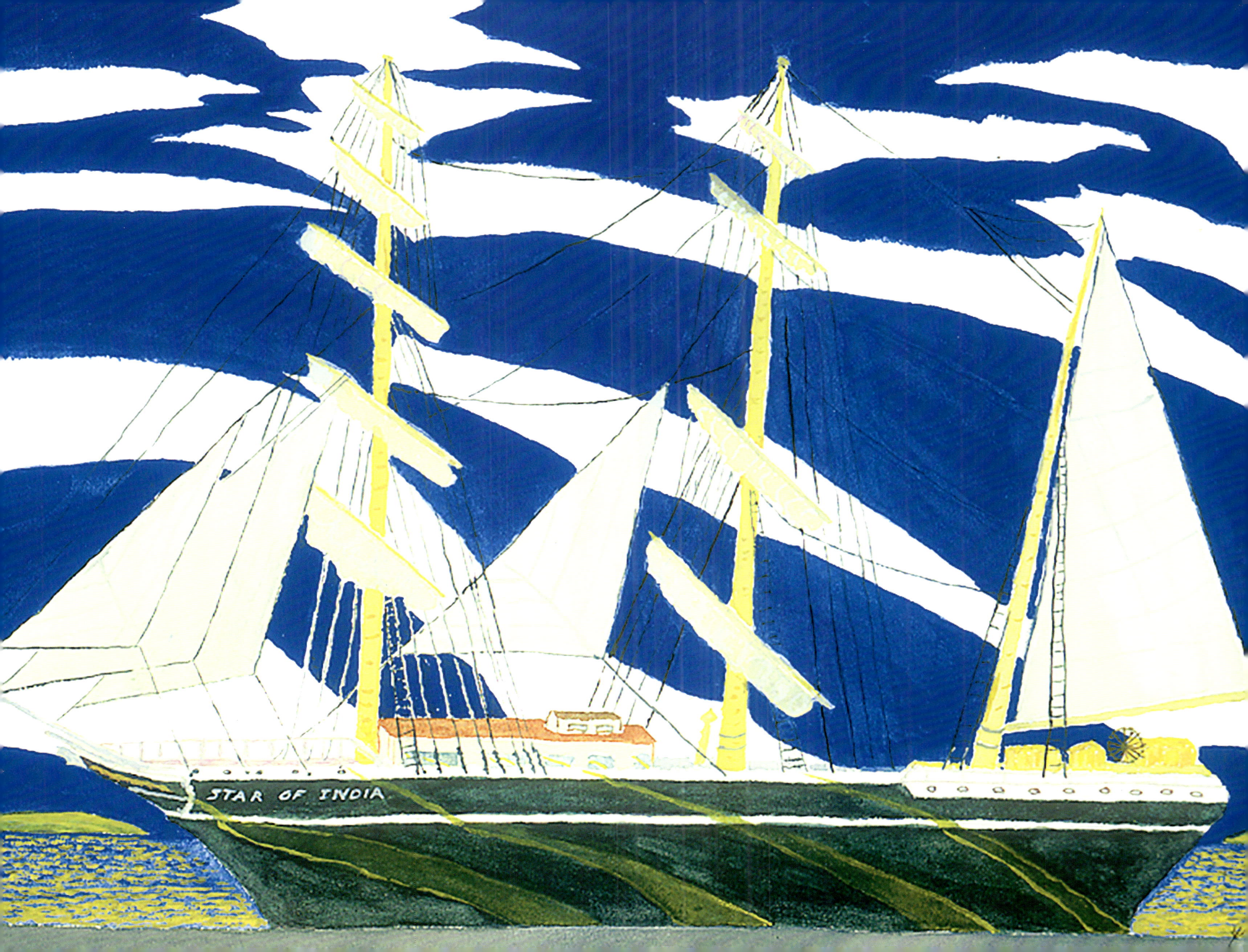
STAR OF INDIA

Notebook to Notebook

The last page
cries out
for a farewell,
or a black-and-white
see you soon –
either way
the next book
awaits,
and the first page
has plenty
to say.